G_{ET} **O**_{VER} *Just* *Yourself!*

Just GET OVER Yourself!

THINK RIGHT. LIVE GREAT.

Anita McCann

Dendy
Publishing & Promotions

To contact the author, Anita McCann, go to www.JustGetOverYourself.com

Published in St. Catharines, Ontario, by Dendy Publishing and Promotions.

Scripture quotations noted NIV are taken from the Holy Bible, New International Version®. NIV®. Copyright © 1973, 1978, 1984 by International Bible Society. Used by permission of Zondervan Publishing House. All rights reserved.

Scripture quotations noted MSG are taken from The Message. Copyright © 1993, 1994, 1995, 1996, 2000, 2001, 2002. Used by permission of NavPress Publishing Group.

Scripture quotations noted NKJV are taken from the New King James Version. Copyright © 1982 by Thomas Nelson, Inc. Used by permission. All rights reserved.

Scripture quotations marked NLT are taken from the Holy Bible, New Living Translation, Copyright © 1996, 2004. Used by permission of Tyndale House Publishers, Inc. Wheaton, Illinois 60189. All rights reserved.

Scripture quotations marked AMP are taken from the Amplified Bible, Copyright © 1954, 1958, 1962, 1964, 1987 by The Lockman Foundation. Used by permission.

Names have been changed to protect the privacy of the individuals mentioned.

Cover and Interior Design by Dendy Publishing and Promotions

Cover Background Photo by Carmen Esau

Cover Photo by Don Hammond/Design Pics Inc.

Back cover author photo by Joanne B. Vink

ISBN-13: 978-0-9865734-0-8

We hope you experience positive life change through this book. Our goal at Dendy Publishing & Promotions is to transform client visions into high-quality products of excellence. We seek to engage truth and offer real-life solutions through books and marketing tools.

Dendy Publishing & Promotions
St. Catharines, ON
www.dendypp.ca

Printed in Ontario, Canada

This book is dedicated to the three most amazing sons a mother could ask for,

Ryan, Conor and Sean.

I will never stop thanking God for your big hearts, bright smiles and wonderful wit. You are a total blessing to me each and every day.

ACKNOWLEDGEMENTS

Five years ago God planted the first seeds of inspiration for this book. It all seemed so simple and straight-forward while the book was in my head. I already knew everything I wanted to put in it, it was simply a matter of putting it on paper...or so I thought! Once I actually started to write, I realized it was going to take a small army to pull it off. God is faithful though, so once I began getting serious, it seemed the right people just began showing up at the right time.

Ruth, thank you for encouraging me to "un-wrap" this project after a long period of neglect. Thank you Dan, Brent, Carmen, Ed, Nancy and Joanne for jumping right onboard and keeping me accountable by continually asking how it was going. Thank you Irene and Heidi for being so enthusiastic and encouraging, and for being great examples of just how powerful these principles are. You are amazing, godly women. Thank you all for catching the vision, and for your persistence and patience.

Ed, thank you for taking all the credit so graciously! You really did give the final push I needed. Carmen and Brent thank you for going to the Bahamas just in time to take the background cover photo. To Karan and Evelyn, you two couldn't possibly be more supportive. Debbie and Wendy at Dendy Publishing and Promotions, you are a dream team for editing, publishing, marketing, cover design and taking care of all the other details I was (and still am) completely clueless about. You are both geniuses.

To my amazing proof readers Debbie, Betty, Evelyn, Kim and Heidi thank you for all the English lessons. I didn't realize how much I needed them until I saw all the red ink. Thank you Adam (and Stephanie) at AE Media for generously providing such an amazing website for this book.

To my family: I could never wish for a better, more caring family than this one. Thank you for always believing in me!

Christine, Mary, Dee, Noeleen, Heather and Raymond, Brian and Dec, just because you're special.

To all my clients, friends and co-workers: thank you for all the inspiration and insight. I have learned so much from each of you.

TABLE OF CONTENTS

Introduction

ree will is amazing when you think about it. It allows you to choose whether to change the things that aren't working in your life or whether to resist change, even if that means continual frustration, failure, disappointment and defeat. Once we realize we have choices in almost every situation, it leaves us without excuses and without a reason to cast blame. God is sovereign, and He has had a plan and purpose for each of us since the beginning of time. However the decision to live that plan is left up to us. It's up to us to let go of the excess baggage we've been carrying and adjust the wrong beliefs and attitudes that keep us stuck and unfulfilled. If we choose to do so, God will give us the power and wisdom to change the one thing that can ultimately change everything: ourselves.

> **Once we realize we have choices in almost every situation, it leaves us without excuses and without a reason to cast blame.**

Several years after becoming a Christian I grew frustrated with not seeing the expected results of living a godly life. At the time I was three thousand miles from home trying to adjust to life in another country. It seemed that my biggest problems just weren't going away no matter what kind of prayers I tried, how much I read the Bible, or how often I went to church. In fact, some problems just kept getting worse. Haggai 1:5-7 effectively summed up my situation: I was sowing much but reaping little, and eating and drinking but remaining unsatisfied.

It soon became crystal clear to me that while a few Christians seemed to have cracked the biblical code for living successfully, so many others were more like me: very far from experiencing success and the abundant life God promised. It seemed we were all searching for authenticity and answers but were having difficulty finding these in churches filled with masquerades of damaged people.

> **We were all searching for authenticity and answers but were having difficulty finding these in churches filled with masquerades of damaged people.**

These first five years of my Christian experience reminded me of the Hebrews' exodus out of Egypt (see Exodus 14 – 17). Even though God provided everything they needed and did many great miracles, yet they resisted Him at every turn. For forty years, these "free" people were going around and around the same mountain experiencing only frustration and no victory. Most ended up dying without ever having experienced what God had promised them. This was not God's plan for them then, and it isn't His plan for us today.

Numbers 32:11-13 tells us that out of these millions who had escaped their captivity in Egypt there were only two who made it to the Promised Land: Joshua and Caleb. What made these two men so different? Unlike the others, Joshua and Caleb believed and obeyed God wholeheartedly. They didn't insist on having things their way as the others did. They seemed to get a hold of God's plan and break loose of any wrong ways of thinking they'd developed in Egypt.

> **Unlike the others, Joshua and Caleb believed and obeyed God wholeheartedly.**

Since I'd had enough of looking at the same old mountains in my life, I told God that I knew there was something else that needed to be done and He was the only one who could show me what it was. Surprisingly He answered my less than reverend request promptly. It wasn't anything I hadn't heard before, but this time the light went on, so to speak. In my spirit I sensed the words "pray and obey". It was quite simple really, but enough to show me that I must be missing something in the obedience department. God's declaration in Hosea 4:6 spoke to me powerfully for the first time:

> *"My people are destroyed for lack of knowledge"*
> *(Hosea 4:6 NKJV).*

I began to realize that even though I was a Christian I had continued to make decisions and tackle problems largely according to my old belief system, occasionally interjecting some new biblical principle I'd learned along the way. I finally recognized that what I really lacked was knowledge and understanding of the ways God had set things up to work; the laws and principles for living He had established from the beginning of creation. I became hopeful that I no longer needed to struggle in my ignorance. I realized His knowledge and understanding were available just for the asking. It was up to me alone to decide how much of them I wanted.

Through my experiences I learned that obedience to God means lining up my beliefs and actions according to His Word. I also discovered that my biggest obstacles to experiencing the promises of God were not the annoying, uncooperative people and circumstances in my life. *It was me.* I realized that my repeated attempts at making excuses, defending myself, or blaming others to one degree or another hadn't worked to bring the change I was looking for, and it never would.

The truth finally dawned on me: the things and people I was trying to blame were largely beyond my ability to change. The one thing I could change was me. While my attention was diverted to what I perceived to be the cause of my problems, I was incapable of seeing what I could change, leaving me to feel like a helpless victim. What I really needed was truth about my own issues, not sympathy, or those well-meaning pat answers that had really gotten me nowhere.

After this revelation, whenever I found myself in a difficult situation I learned to ask God to show me where I was going wrong and what to do about it. Little by little I learned how things looked from His kingdom perspective, though I rarely – if ever – liked what I saw. The amazing thing was that as I learned these truths and made adjustments in my thinking and attitudes, I just kept getting freer and happier!

After having seen areas of my own life and the lives of many others radically transformed by understanding these biblical keys, I know one thing with absolute certainty: His truth is the only thing that can set us free in every way. His Word brings healing and *"delivers us from…destruction"* (Psalm 107:20 NKJV). It frees us from the wrong expectations we place on God and others. It heals us from the wounds of the past, and frees us from fear of the future. It frees us from having to believe the lies that have blinded us from His truth and shaped us into unhappy, frustrated Christians.

Allowing God to reveal our true beliefs and motives can be a scary prospect. We are all afraid of what might happen when the truth is exposed. But God is all about life and goodness! He only wants to remove the things that are keeping us from fulfilling His purpose and experiencing His best. Seeing what's been hiding in our hearts isn't pretty or comfortable, but it is powerful. It also helps us see just how unconditional God's love is for us. We need to pray with the Psalmist,

*Search me, O God, and know my heart; test me and
know my anxious thoughts. See if there is any
offensive way in me, and lead me in the way everlasting
(Psalm 139:23-24 NIV).*

Remember, none of it was ever hidden from Him anyway!

We may not need a miracle to change our circumstances after all, just a reality check and understanding of how the kingdom of God operates in our lives. Its laws and principles are very different from the world's way of doing things.

We need a change in our beliefs to realize that we contribute significantly to the problems we face. Our core beliefs actually determine our success or failure in every area of our life, including our finances, our health, and our relationships. Unless we are aware of wrong beliefs and get honest about our real motivations, true lasting heart-change is unlikely.

Each of us has a history of challenges and difficulties which causes us to view life through lenses tainted with a mixture of pain, fear, pride and shame. Our skewed perception makes it difficult to be objective and honest with ourselves about our contribution to the problems we've encountered. Some of the difficult situations we face are unavoidable, perhaps the result of the sinful, selfish choices of others, or just circumstances that are beyond our control. The truth is that even under difficult circumstances we can still choose a righteous attitude. Rather than wasting the time and pain these experience have cost us, we can allow them to refine our character and use them as stepping stones to freedom and success.

The choice to be successful in life belongs to us. We can continue to avoid taking responsibility for our actions and persist in blaming others. If we do however, self righteousness, stubborn pride, and our determination to be right will cause us to miss valuable opportunities to grow and learn from our past mistakes. The only alternative is to become bitter, remain stuck, continue to experience failure and miss out on the blessings of trust and obedience.

If you are tired of settling for less than God's best, this book is for you. In the following chapters you will discover common areas of wrong beliefs and attitudes that have kept many from experiencing freedom and success God's way. As you allow God to expose these areas in your life you will learn how to effectively replace areas of deceit with the truth of who God created you to be. You don't have to waste another minute; it's time to discover God's unique success plan for your life as it is clearly laid out in the book of Joshua:

> *This Book of the Law shall not depart out of your mouth, but you shall meditate on it day and night, that you may observe and do according to all that is written in it. For then you shall make your way prosperous, and then you shall deal wisely and have good success (Joshua 1:8 AMP).*

What follows are four recommendations to help you meditate on God's Word as this verse suggests. They will help you experience even more radical change as you read this book.

1. Read one chapter of this book daily for the next forty days.

2. Choose one habit that is keeping your life out of balance and "fast" it (or *give it up*) as you read through this book. It will be something that takes up your valuable time and energy and draws your attention away from God. I suggest praying and allowing God to show it to you. Here are some examples of things people have fasted: frivolous or impulse spending, watching television, listening to the radio, reading anything other than the Bible (and of course, this book), playing computer games, speaking negatively,

gossiping, judging, drinking alcohol, hanging out with negative people, and unnecessarily talking on the phone. Remember that the purpose of fasting is to give the time and attention you'll gain to God and prayer.

3. Record any new truth God reveals to you. It might be something that you've read, experienced or heard that got your attention. It may be as little as one point per day.

4. Make the effort to read any recommended Scriptures and expand on reading the ones you will find on these pages.

Part One

Exposing the Mind

*So here's what I want you to do, God helping
you: take your everyday, ordinary life — your
sleeping, eating, going-to-work, and walking-around
life — and place it before God as an offering.
Embracing what God does for you is the best thing
you can do for him.*

*Don't become so well-adjusted to your culture
that you fit into it without even thinking. Instead,
fix your attention on God. You'll be changed from
the inside out.*

*Readily recognize what he wants from you, and
quickly respond to it. Unlike the culture around
you, always dragging you down to its level of
immaturity, God brings the best out of you, develops
well-formed maturity in you.*
(Romans 12:2 MSG)

Chapter 1

KINGDOM KNOWLEDGE

For he has rescued us from the kingdom of darkness and
transferred us into the Kingdom of his dear Son.

COLOSSIANS 1:13

As believers we have access to God's kingdom of truth. However, unless our minds are renewed to the ways of this new kingdom we will continue to function under old belief systems. We will only be able to experience God's kingdom privileges and power to the degree that our hearts and lives are submitted to His rule. Salvation brings us into the kingdom of God, but until we gain knowledge of how His supernatural kingdom operates, we will be limited in the way we experience His power in our lives. God's truth carries the power to break through any deception that has kept us from living freely.

If you've ever seen an animal or person that's been rescued from an abusive situation, you'll know that simply placing them in a better environment cannot immediately wipe away the pain, fear and negative conditioning that those years of abuse have inflicted on them. We are the same way when we come into God's kingdom. Even if we have not suffered obvious abuse, we've likely been conditioned to a way of thinking that cannot comprehend the depth of God's love for us, or the supernatural power He has made available to us to accomplish His purposes.

God has a system of kingdom rules and laws that many Christians have scant knowledge of, yet Jesus spoke of the kingdom of God wherever He went. God wants us to have the keys to righteous living so we can be positioned for our God-ordained destiny. A faulty belief system cannot get us there, but it can be corrected by *"seeking first [God's] kingdom and its righteousness"* (Matt 6:33). At the end of this verse Jesus adds the promise that everything else shall be given to the believer as well, as the result of a whole-hearted seeking after God.

The verse from Matthew 6 shows clearly that seeking the kingdom of God and His righteousness are to be the believer's number one priority. If you are like me, you used to think the number one priority was to be something else, such as evangelizing, preaching, or going to the mission field.

> **God really wants us to be whole, but He can't get us there without first getting our attention, cooperation, obedience and trust.**

Read the Gospel of Matthew over again, this time highlighting the word "kingdom" every time you see it. I had never realized how much Jesus actually spoke of the kingdom of God until I did this. The kingdom appeared to be a central theme of His ministry. Since it was so important to Him, it should be to us as well.

The reason many of us in the Church are unaware of God's kingdom principles is that we lack knowledge and understanding of His Word. God has given us His Word and we get to choose when and how much to read it. In addition to giving us His Word, He has also told us that He is available to communicate with us 24/7, so we get to choose when and what to pray about. We can even choose to stick our fingers in our ears or shut our eyes to His truth. God really wants us to be whole, but He can't get us there without first getting our attention, cooperation, obedience and trust. Then He will give us all the wisdom we ask for, so we can access what we need. Jesus says,

> *See how every student well-trained in God's kingdom*
> *is like the owner of a general store who can put his*
> *hands on anything you need, old or new, exactly when*
> *you need it (Matt. 13:52 MSG).*

Imagine being able to put your hand on whatever truth and direction you need, when you need it!

In discovering God's kingdom we find our true purpose. God has not been hiding it from us. Our own lack of ability to see truth gets in the way. We need knowledge of God's Word to know God's will. When we know His will we can obey Him. God has given us the keys of truth and when we apply them we will begin to see situations change. Jesus tells His disciples,

> *I will give you the keys of the kingdom of heaven; and*
> *whatever you bind (declare to be improper and*
> *unlawful) on earth must be what is already bound in*
> *heaven; and whatever you loose (declare lawful) on*
> *earth must be what is already loosed in heaven (Matt.*
> *16:19 AMP).*

What if your failure to deal with the issues God wants you to address is the cause of your personal struggles? Wouldn't you dig into the Bible if you truly believed the solutions to your problems could be found there? Jesus tells the parable of a man who finds a treasure buried in a field and promptly goes out to sell everything he has so he can buy the field and claim the treasure. He goes on to liken the kingdom of heaven to a pearl dealer who finds a single, breathtakingly beautiful pearl and subsequently sells everything he has to acquire the pearl (Matt. 13:44-46). To the seekers in Jesus' parable, the treasure (the keys to kingdom living) was worth everything they owned, and they parted with it gladly. Is it worth everything to you to discover the keys to kingdom living in the Bible?

As believers we are all called to advance the kingdom of God on the earth. Each of us has a specific role in the body of Christ; a unique way of fulfilling our calling. You can't know what your role is until God reveals it to you, and you can't be equipped to fulfill it unless you submit your will to His. I guarantee that you will never be happier or more successful than when you discover and live the will of God for your life. God is longing for you to do this!

I've seen too many people remain stuck in life because of the lies they allow themselves to believe, just like I did. Even when the truth is right in front of us we resist it because humility doesn't come easily. It's hard to admit when we are wrong until we realize that this may be the very thing that prevents us from freely enjoying life.

When we give control to God He can use even the dumbest things we've done for His glory! The insights God taught me while working through my own failures and foolishness have prepared and equipped me to help other people to see their problems for what they really are while pointing them to God's solutions. When people become open to hearing and accepting truth, there is no situation God can't change. My passion is helping people succeed in reaching their potential and fulfilling their God-given destiny. I didn't have anyone else in mind when I started, I just wanted *me* fixed!

When we give control to God He can use even the dumbest things we've done for His glory!

God doesn't waste anything! In fact He multiplies everything. While fixing *me* is an ongoing process, I have personally seen these same principles transform other people's lives, relationships, health, and finances. I love to witness what happens when the penny drops and the lights go on. In an instant, years of confusion and hopelessness can suddenly disappear as the light of truth reveals problems for what they really are. I've seen God turn too many seemingly impossible situations around to believe He won't do it for you too.

There are obstacles that each of us have to overcome in order to understand and experience kingdom life as God intends. Entrance to God's kingdom began with repentance, and advancement within the kingdom is also determined by ongoing repentance. Before Jesus even arrived on the scene John the Baptist was preparing people for the kingdom of Heaven by calling them to repentance (Matt. 3:2). If you can't recognize and admit your sins, you will remain stuck in life.

In the following chapters, you will have many opportunities to get honest and real with yourself and God. Trusting Him is the key to living to your maximum potential.

"Trust God from the bottom of your heart; don't try to figure out everything on your own. Listen for God's voice in everything you do, everywhere you go; he's the one who will keep you on track. Don't assume that you know it all. Run to God! Run from evil! Your body will glow with health, your very bones will vibrate with life!"

Proverbs 3:5-7 MSG

What you know determines where and how far you will go! Challenge yourself by committing to read the gospels over the next few weeks, highlighting the word "kingdom" everywhere you see it.

Chapter 2

PROBLEMS

*The [uncompromisingly] righteous is delivered out of
trouble and the wicked gets into it instead.*

PROVERBS 11:8 AMP

Problems hurt. Hurting people are everywhere and they all handle problems differently. Some people deal with their problems by overeating, drinking or shopping 'til they drop. Others use drugs, or escape into the fantasy world of television or computer games. Many try to bury themselves in countless hours of work. These are all ways of avoiding the reality of why our problems exist, and they represent an attempt to escape from asking ourselves the really hard question, "am I suffering for doing what is right, or as a result my own wrong choices?"

Let us first look at how some of our problems were created. Some of the experiences and influences we've been exposed to have programmed us with false information about who we are, moulding within us a faulty self image.

This can result in feelings of unworthiness and inadequacy. The resulting shame and guilt causes us to build strongholds to protect ourselves from further hurt, but in reality, these walls also shut out the very truth we need in order to be free. The walls of these strongholds are reinforced every time we make excuses, deny, blame

> **Most Christians would agree that God has the answer to every problem. Why then do our lives not reflect this?**

others, or justify our poor choices and behaviors. We become increasingly blinded to seeing and accepting the truth about ourselves, which also keeps us from receiving the truth and forgiveness of God that we need in order to be free. This is often the reason behind some of the persistent problems we experience.

Problems are all around us in the workplace, the marketplace, and at home. We struggle with finances, our health, and our relationships. Solutions are out there, but we may have trouble finding them because of obstacles that get in our way. In this book we will deal with the obstacles of our reluctance to take responsibility for our own poor choices and behaviors.

Most Christians would agree that God has the answer to every problem. Why then do our lives not reflect this? Many of us are caught in vicious negative cycles in our relationships, our finances, and our physical and emotional health. These problems just don't seem to go away no matter how much we try to solve them. We may eventually come to the conclusion that the problem is just not going away because God actually put it there to teach us some kind of lesson, therefore we might as well accept it and stop trying. Could it be that these problems can't be solved because we haven't recognized the real causes behind them, the real reasons why we remain stuck?

Like stubborn stains, some problems in life just seem impossible to get rid of no matter which solution we apply. In our frustration we quickly point out that the Apostle

Paul also had a thorn in the flesh that God didn't remove (2 Cor. 12:7), forgetting that this is the same God who opened up the Red Sea, raised the dead, healed the lepers, the blind, and fed thousands with a little boy's lunch! So wouldn't it be better to go through life believing that God is not purposely keeping anything good from us?

Paul's issue certainly didn't hinder him from successfully fulfilling his destiny. But there were a few million people who died in the desert without ever having seen God's promises realized. Most of the Israelites spent their final forty years in the desert because they had determined what the solutions to their hardships should be. They based them on beliefs shaped by their former experiences, not on their knowledge of God.

God's answers just did not fit in with their plan of how things should be fixed. His solutions were not complicated. They were simple: obey, take responsibility, repent when you do wrong, and maintain an attitude of thanksgiving.

Is it possible that we also have wrong beliefs resulting from past experiences that blind us from seeing and accepting God's solutions? The Hebrews resisted God because they wanted things their way. They didn't want to change the one thing that needed to change, the one thing that they actually could change: themselves, with all their wrong beliefs and destructive attitudes. They preferred to use blaming and complaining to get the heat off of themselves. If you haven't already done so, read the book of Exodus in order to see how well it worked for them. Know that with the same behaviour you will get the same results they did: a life of frustration, confusion and unfulfilled destiny.

Sometimes the stubborn problems we face are very much within our ability to resolve. The Christian life is all

> **Is it possible that we also have wrong beliefs resulting from past experiences that blind us from seeing and accepting God's solutions?**

about us doing our part and letting God do His. From time to time we all lose sight of the plot because we take our eyes off God and try to come up with our own solutions. We need to be careful not to make the decision to accept our problems as God's will without first consulting God.

By this time you have probably viewed your stubborn problems from every angle except the God angle. God sees the whole problem while you examine it bit by bit, never quite being able to see the whole thing at once. He not only sees it all, He also knows what attitude or wrong belief you hold that is keeping it there.

If you have stubborn problems that are consuming time, money and attention, and damaging relationships or health, chances are that you've been searching for answers in the wrong places. It may not be the annoying people in your life or the "economic climate" that have kept you from experiencing breakthroughs or success.

The interesting thing is that every single Christian would readily admit that they are sinners, but when asked specifically about their sin most have trouble finding a real one to own up to. They may admit to a little impatience, frustration or lack of self discipline, but seldom seem to see the pride, fear or selfishness that is behind their presenting problems.

> **I have personally discovered that it is always easier for us to confess someone else's sin than our own.**

I have personally discovered that it is always easier for us to confess someone else's sin than our own. This helps us avoid the discomfort of dealing with any fear, shame or insecurity we may be hiding, and even appears to make life easier by getting the heat off us and onto someone else. We may also experience the added benefits of sympathy and support because then we can be the victim.

This is not to say that sympathy and support are never appropriate - they certainly are - but there is a human tendency to remain the victim for longer than is good for us. Making excuses, blaming others and craving sympathy will keep us stuck in our problems. The first thing we must decide then, is whether we really want solutions for our problems if that means taking responsibility for them, or whether we would rather continue to bask in sympathy. Is your need to be right and appear guiltless more important than your need to be free?

Problems are not always what they first appear to be. If we have a distorted view of our problems, it is impossible to find the right solution. Debt is not always the result of not having enough money. It may be the result of foolish spending choices, or impatience to get the latest "thing". Sickness is not always a physical problem. Poor choices can lead to stress and stress is a common factor in several serious health conditions. Poor lifestyle and eating choices are also behind many health issues. Loneliness is not always the result of other people's lack of concern for us. Sometimes we may adopt negative attitudes that others just can't be around, or perhaps we are unwilling to accept opportunities to get involved because it demands something of us. If we have distorted views of problems, we will not find the right solutions.

If we have a distorted view of our problems, it is impossible to find the right solution.

Sometimes we become victims of our own choices, denying reality and refusing to accept loving truth. Often truth about the real cause of our problems eludes us because we do not want to believe that our problem may be the result of something we are doing wrong. This in turn causes us to interpret the problem incorrectly.

Our biggest problem, frequently, is how we see the problem. Destructive problems can't be solved with only the knowledge that we had at the time we caused or allowed them to develop. Ignorance of God's ways brings problems. We need knowledge of God's truth – His kingdom solutions – to help us understand how we can move beyond the frustrations that keep us stuck. Hosea helps us see how critical it is to have the right information. In chapter 4 of Hosea God says through His prophet, *"My people are destroyed for lack of knowledge; because you [the priestly nation] have rejected knowledge"* (Hosea 4:6 AMP).

God has solutions for our real problems. It isn't good enough for Him to rid us of just our surface issues. God isn't into behavior modification, He wants radical transformation. He wants the solutions to be permanent, so that we don't struggle with the same issues over and over again. He does not want us to lose one job after another, go from one abusive relationship to another, or to be broke month after month. Real solutions to deep-rooted problems require major surgery, not just a little band-aid!

Finding the right answers means knowing what His Word says about our problems and allowing Him to reveal the strategy for overcoming them. God gives us access to everything we need to live right. Overcoming our own problems God's way is one of the ways in which we are empowered to help others solve theirs. Human problems are no match for God's solutions!

> *"His divine power has given to us all things that pertain to life and godliness, through the knowledge of Him who called us by glory and virtue."*
>
> *2 Peter 1:3 NKJV*

W hen you deny it, you buy it...but it's doubtful anyone else does.

Chapter 3

DELUSIONS

"The Lord opens the eyes of the blind, the Lord lifts up those who are bowed down, the Lord loves the [uncompromisingly] righteous (those upright in heart and in right standing with Him)".

PSALM 146:8 AMP

Have you ever seen a man with a really bad comb-over? You know, the poor guy who has lost eighty percent of his hair and grows one side long enough to comb over and cover the baldness? It doesn't really fool anyone, does it? We all know that he's trying to hide the fact that there really isn't any hair under there. The problem is that he is the only one that is fooled.

Even those of us with a full head of hair have learned methods of covering up. We hide things that we believe are missing on the inside, areas of insecurity or inadequacy. Just like the bald guy, none of us would like it if someone tried to flip the hair back to expose what's underneath. The real problem is not the baldness; it's the fear of what people would think if they could see the truth.

All of us have things that we are desperately trying to hide. We may not even be conscious of what they are. Strangely, it is always easier to see what another person is attempting to hide rather than what we ourselves are hiding. Shame and guilt force us to develop ways to cover up and defend our real selves. Our fears prevent us from experiencing true intimacy within relationships, even in our relationship with God.

> **Strangely, it is always easier to see what another person is attempting to hide rather than what we ourselves are hiding.**

The ability to see clearly how and why God created us is essential to achieving wholeness. We know that we are each unique and different in our gifting, talents, appearance, and personality. God put us together with great care, and knew us before we were even a seed in our mother's womb! He even knows the number of hairs on our head, and cares just as much for those who have a lot as for those who don't have many left!

Living in a fallen world and dealing with our own sin nature often makes it difficult to determine God's direction. God says our own hearts deceive us; people deceive us and Satan (the father of lies) deceives us. His purpose is to continually bombard us with lies, knowing that the result of our accepting and believing them will lead to our failure and destruction. Because we are surrounded by deception we struggle to know and understand God's truth.

Most believers desire to live right and to obey God, knowing that we will not do it perfectly. We become frustrated when we have done all we know to do and still circumstances, relationships and issues of all kinds seem impossible to change.

Many people who go for counseling ask for help, but really believe they have tried all there is to try and there's nothing more they can do. They hope a counselor will be able to point out the real source of the problem – as long as it's not them! Most really want someone to agree that it is all someone else's fault, and that it is okay to give up, find another husband, change jobs, or move to another city to get away from the problem. They also look for someone to blame when they find their new plan doesn't work. For some, counseling is often the last resort, so they can truly say they have tried everything and now have permission to give up.

People believe that change in their situation is out of their control because So-and-So just won't stop_____ (you can fill in the blank), and they are obviously NEVER going to change! Just try suggesting to the person who knows it all, has done it all, has been-there, seen the movie and bought the t-shirt, that God may have a few ideas they haven't tried yet, then

Trying to change others won't ever work and will always make things worse.

sit back and watch the sparks fly! The real truth of the matter is that we are the only person we can change. Trying to change others won't ever work and will always make things worse. If we can't accept that our way of doing things is flawed, it is difficult for God to communicate with us because we've closed the door and bolted it from the inside! Proverbs tells us that "there is a way that seems right unto man but in the end it leads to death (Prov. 14: 12 NIV). Being convinced that we are right doesn't help us escape consequences.

It takes humility to accept that if we continue to insist on seeing and doing things our way, it will lead to death; the death of relationships, opportunities, dreams and hope. If you have trouble understanding this, just think of a marriage where both spouses just can't get along because they both believe their way is the only right way. They think they are responsible to confess each other's sin, ignoring their own in the process. What do you think are the odds that a relationship like this will last? Jesus addresses the problem of fault finding this way,

> *...Or how can you say to your brother, "Brother, allow me to take out the speck that is in your eye," when you yourself do not see the beam that is in your own eye? You actor (pretender, hypocrite)! First take the beam out of your own eye, and then you will see clearly to take out the speck that is in your brother's eye (Luke 6:42 AMP).*

When the Bible talks about getting the beam out of our own eye before we can deal with our brother's speck, it is saying that there is a lot about ourselves that we cannot see. What we cannot see is interfering with – or *marring* – our perception of people and situations. Think about how dangerous it is to ignore the little blind spots in our vehicle while driving. Now think of how dangerous it is to go through life with a beam in your eye!

The problem with blind spots is that they get in the way of our seeking out and receiving the truth that we need in order to experience life as God intended. Before we can start to deal with our blind spots, we have to humble ourselves and acknowledge that they do, in fact, exist. These blind spots have a tendency to lurk behind layers of defenses built over a lifetime of hurt, betrayal and disappointment. It's not comfortable or easy to go there. If we want to experience true freedom though, avoidance is no longer an option.

Before we can start to deal with our blind spots, we have to humble ourselves and acknowledge that they do, in fact, exist.

None of us have difficulty seeing the blind spots of others; seeing our own is the real challenge. Realize that everyone who is close to us already sees some of what we think we are hiding, so we really are the only ones deceived.

Try to imagine a room full of people with two-by-fours protruding out of an eye socket. Obviously these people cannot get close to each other. We have all learned to tip-toe around each other's blind spots so we don't rock the boat. We can't get close to each other, and then wonder why we do not experience real intimacy in our relationships!

Dare to ask yourself who you really are when your defenses and pretenses are laid down. Ultimately, the only true picture we need of ourselves is how God sees us. This process requires a commitment to openness, which may not always be easy, and we won't always like what we hear or see.

> **The key to understanding deception is to realize that when we are deceived about something, we don't know it.**

Remember, the only alternative is to stay the way we are, struggling with the same kind of frustrations day-in and day-out, blinded to the truth that will set us free.

The dictionary defines a blind spot as an area that cannot be observed under existing circumstances. Obviously there needs to be a change in existing circumstances before we can see what we are hiding.

The key to understanding deception is to realize that when we are deceived about something, we don't know it. God has given us several ways to stay out of this trap: by staying close to Him, by knowing His truth, and by seeking accountability within relationships. Overcoming this problem is always a two-sided process. First we must realize that hyper-sensitivity, pride, stubbornness and defensiveness, keep us from receiving truth. Second we must understand that fear, reasoning, and self-preservation will keep us from speaking truth. We are

> **Jesus always loved, but He never enabled anyone's weaknesses by compromising truth.**

all perishing in blindness to the degree that our relationships lack loving truth.

If all this sounds a little tough, it may be because we are well aware that we are a long way from expressing loving truth in our relationships. We may also be a little bit afraid of what we might hear or have to say if we decide to go with it. Understand that holding back truth also prevents us from gaining insight into our good qualities! Remember what happened to the woman at the well when Jesus pointed out her less-than-lovely history and ungodly lifestyle?

> *"I have no husband," she said. "That's nicely put: 'I have no husband.' You've had five husbands, and the man you're living with now isn't even your husband. You spoke the truth there, sure enough" (John 4:17-18 MSG).*

Instead of feeling crushed, (as I would have expected) she was excited that someone could know everything about her and still love and accept her! She received and accepted what Jesus said and it changed her forever. She could have chosen to become offended and defensive and stay the way she was, yet she went back to her village and raved,

> *"Come see a man who knew all about the things I did, who knows me inside and out. Do you think this could be the Messiah?" And they went out to see for themselves (John 4:28:30 MSG).*

Look at the results of just one person accepting the truth about herself! Because of this one woman's humility many more Samaritans committed themselves to faith in Jesus. Jesus always loved, but He never enabled anyone's weaknesses by compromising truth. He knows us inside and out, and wants to show us what He sees so we can be free! We are responsible to have the beams removed from our own eyes.

The amazing thing is that when we've dealt honestly and humbly with our own beams we are empowered to help others see theirs, because having seen our own sin we no longer feel compelled to judge others in theirs. We can speak the truth in love because we ourselves have experienced the freedom that it brings.

If believers could learn how to speak the truth and receive loving truth from each other humbly, I believe it would transform the body and remove much of the confusion over why believers struggle so much in ways God never intended.

American Idol, a popular television talent show, presents many good examples of people who have probably never had anyone be honest with them about their lack of talent. There they are, on screen in front of millions of viewers, likely being told for the first time by judges who are complete strangers that they don't have an ounce of talent. If we love people enough, we have the responsibility to tell them the truth gently and lovingly when the opportunity arises; otherwise, we set them up for humiliating and painful experiences further down life's road.

> **If believers could learn how to speak the truth and receive loving truth from each other humbly, I believe it would transform the body.**

Here are a few examples to get you thinking:

You have a strong-willed, opinionated friend who criticizes her boss and co-workers continually. She is openly disrespectful and comes to you complaining that she has been passed over for promotion time after time. Do you gently and lovingly suggest that she prayerfully bring her critical attitude before God, or do you agree with her that she has been a victim of favoritism?

Do you listen to friends repeatedly complain about their spouse without ever pointing out what the Bible says about how they are to love and respect them? This includes not magnifying their quirks and faults. Are you responsibly helping them to focus on the strengths of their partner, or do you agree with them, helping them justify their false sense of righteousness, further decreasing their level of satisfaction in the marriage?

What if your friend complains that her child's teacher is always picking on him for no reason? You've regularly volunteered in the classroom and see that he is certainly not the angel his mother thinks he is. In fact, he is the worst behaved kid in the class! Are you lovingly honest with her? To withhold truth from her actually makes you partly responsible for her growing anger and resentment towards all the wrong people. Worse still, she is robbed of the opportunity to deal with her child's issues before they become worse.

Are you willing to be the kind of friend/Christian who risks offending others for their benefit? Or will you continue to hope that someone else more confrontational will take responsibility and do it? You may be the one God has placed there to gently point things out along the way so that an all-out confrontation never becomes necessary. Sooner or later, we all will get the truth. It can come in many forms: delinquency, divorce, rejection, prison, bankruptcy, abuse or even hell. If you believed loving truth spoken in season could prevent some of these unfortunate outcomes, would you risk it?

If you believed loving truth spoken in season could prevent some unfortunate outcomes, would you risk it?

Real love looks for and hopes for the best in people and situations. When our communication does not reflect this kind of love, it is not accomplishing God's purpose of accountability in relationships. Authentic love will not let us or others remain victims of choices made because of wrong beliefs and perceptions.

Thankfully there is some evidence in today's culture that truth is still valued. Dr. Phil and Judge Judy are some examples of that. The world rejoices when justice is done and the truth is spoken…but of course, only as long as it is not directed at ME! We enjoy watching other people having their specks removed and secretly hope that with all the attention focused on them, no one is noticing our beam!

Are you ready and willing to discover what has been blindsiding you? Open your mind and heart to God and those who love you enough to tell you the truth, and you will be set free. Getting defensive and touchy when something hits too close to the truth is often a good indication of where our blind spots and delusions are hiding. The reality is that those close to us have probably hinted a dozen different ways at some issue we have, but we haven't been able to see or accept it because we immediately race to our own defense or resort to denial. If you want truth, change your response, decide to remain open and listen and ask yourself what it would mean if this was actually true of you. This is where the blinders begin to come off!

Are you ready and willing to discover what has been blindsiding you?

"I will bring the blind by a way they did not know; I will lead them in paths they have not known. I will make darkness light before them and crooked places straight. These things I will do for them, and not forsake them."

Isaiah 42:16 NKJV

Feedback is the food of champions! You need truth to be free from all delusions.

Chapter 4

BELIEFS

He who refuses and ignores instruction and correction despises himself, but he who heeds reproof gets understanding.

PROVERBS 15:32 AMP

Radical life change is not accidental. It requires making decisions and then acting on them. Where we are today is the result of acting on past decisions we've made. Among other things we decided who to marry, where to work and where to live. The decisions we've made are based on what we believe. Even if we believe we have arrived at our current situation in life because of the persuasion or manipulation of others, we have to accept that at some point we agreed to go along with their plan. Some part of us believed it was the thing to do. Perhaps we didn't trust our own instincts or believed others knew better than us. We may even have believed that not cooperating with them would have made life more difficult.

When it comes to relationships with others, our beliefs about ourselves will determine how we act and how we interpret their words and actions. If we believe that we are attractive, intelligent and likeable, we will approach others with confidence. If we see ourselves as boring and unappealing, with nothing to contribute, it is likely that we will shy away from contact, believing that others do not want to be around us. What we believe about ourselves also determines how we allow people to treat us, and how we in turn choose to treat them! It stands to reason then, that lasting change in any area is only possible if our deeply rooted erroneous beliefs are changed.

Changed beliefs are evidenced by changed behaviour.

Henry Ford once said "If you think you can or you think you can't, you are right". Clearly what we think and believe may become our reality. This statement is confirmed in the following nugget of wisdom from Proverbs:

> "*...For as he thinks in his heart, so is he*" (*Prov. 23:7 NKJV*)..

Obviously this means we must change our internal beliefs at their core before it is possible to have real lasting change in our behaviour. Changed beliefs are evidenced by changed behaviour. Galatians 5:19-21 describes what kind of fruit we can expect if we continue to follow our sin nature: immorality, impurity, sensuality, idolatry, sorcery, enmities, strife, jealousy, outbursts of anger, disputes, dissensions, factions, envying, drunkenness [and] carousing. The fruit (the behaviour or results) of a new life in Christ is quite the opposite: "*...the fruit of the spirit is love, joy, peace, longsuffering, kindness, goodness, faithfulness, gentleness and self control* " (Gal. 5:22-23 NKJV).

We can choose the kind of results or fruit we want to develop and produce in our lives.

In today's world, change is big business. People want change; there is no question about that. Unhappy or dissatisfied with their current circumstances people spend billions on what they believe will be quick fixes. According to *Market Data* research, the U.S. Weight Loss & Diet Control Market is estimated to have reached over $60 billion in 2008! The popularity of cosmetic surgery also continues to grow. In 2009 the American Society of Plastic Surgeons statistics showed a 69% increase in profit compared to 2000![1] It seems the easier the methods appear, the more popular they become. People are prepared to pay more for fast, painless, and effortless results. Even though the failure rate of dieting is well documented, people continue to buy into it, easily handing over their hard earned dollars, fully aware of the cold, hard facts. How can this be? People want a fast and easy fix. Only when they experience failure does their belief in a fast fix begin to change.

Why do their beliefs not work in this situation? For one thing, people's beliefs begin to change when the rules and restrictions become too difficult to maintain. Some studies show that it takes over forty attempts at dieting before weight loss is permanent! Is it possible that after all those attempts people's beliefs finally conform to the truth? Could it be that we don't allow our wrong beliefs and self perceptions to be transformed? The truth may also be presented by a doctor's order to "change your habits or risk premature death". Until people accept the real truth, it seems that many believe they can escape the negative consequences of their poor habits: smoking, drinking, drugs, and promiscuity, just to name a few. If change is to last, it is vital that wrong beliefs be replaced by permanent unchanging truth.

> **According to Market Data research, the U.S. Weight Loss & Diet Control Market is estimated to have reached over $60 billion in 2008.**

We must understand that just believing something does not make it true. Truth is truth whether we choose to believe it or not.

Everybody believes in something. Beliefs, whether or not they are based in truth will become the driving force of our life. Eve believed in God; she didn't even need faith to do it because she could see God with her natural eyes. Satan knew he couldn't stop her believing in God, so his only hope of getting mankind off track was to convince her that even though God was real, He was withholding something good from her, something she believed she needed in order to be fulfilled. It is this same belief that leads us astray today. We satisfy our own appetites with things that will ultimately lead to our destruction because we don't really believe that God wants to satisfy all our desires.

> **Beliefs, whether or not they are based in truth, will become the driving force in our life.**

Belief is the basis of action. We will act according to what we believe. If in our relationship with God we believe that He is good and loving, we will approach Him differently than someone who believes Him to be a harsh judge just waiting for them to fail so He can punish them.

The problem with the tree of the knowledge was that eating its fruit meant that man would know (experience) both good and evil. God did not want that for His children. He did not want us to know the evils of murder, rape, war, famine, disease, divorce, broken relationships, and abuses of all kinds. While all of us have experienced the impact of evil, believing in God's goodness restores our hope for a different outcome, just as it did for King David. He wrote, *"What, would have become of me had I not believed to see the Lord's goodness in the land of the living!"* (Psalm 27:13 AMP).

Why is it that some people are successful in life (often despite the odds being stacked against them) while others who are equally (or more) beautiful, talented or intelligent never succeed at all? The difference is often that the ones who succeed believe in their own ability and talent enough to stay the course and never give up.

Think how much more can be achieved by a person who believes in the vision and destiny that God has for them! If we will grasp the truth about God's plans for us and believe them, working together with God we will achieve them!

In the last chapter we learned how to uncover our blind spots (our areas of deception) by replacing them with God's truth. His truth will transform us into the people He intended us to be, and help us to successfully fulfill His destiny and purpose.

We each have a choice: we can make excuses and stay where we are, or commit to allowing God to transform our beliefs. As a result we can experience the abundant life Jesus died to give us.

> *"Throw off your old sinful nature and your former way*
> *of life, which is corrupted by lust and deception.*
> *Instead, let the Spirit renew your thoughts and*
> *attitudes."*
>
> *Ephesians 4:22-23 NLT*

You will live according to what you believe; you alone are responsible for what you believe.

Chapter 5

INFLUENCES

He who walks [as a companion] with wise men is wise,
but he who associates with [self-confident] fools is [a fool
himself and] shall smart for it.

PROVERBS 13:20 AMP

It is doubtful that anyone reading this has escaped the impact of another person's negative choices or behaviors. We have all been victims to some degree. Some may have been victim of horrific sexual, physical and emotional abuse, others to gossip, rejection or betrayal. This book is not an attempt to minimize events of the past which have caused great pain and brokenness. It *does* seek to provide kingdom keys for overcoming a victim mentality, which can result from such abuse. A victim mentality limits our experience and joy in life even long after the victimization has ended, and it causes us to accept and believe false information about our circumstances and ourselves.

Someone with a victim mentality often believes that change is impossible because their abuser still holds the reins. Victims believe that they have no power to change, but God sees it differently and tells us that Jesus came to set us free from the power these lies have over us! In John 10:10 Jesus contrasts His gift of abundant life with the destructive work of the thief, who comes only to steal, kill and destroy (John 10:10 NKJV).

Through victimization we have been lied to and have learned to expect the worst. Mistakenly, we adopt the mentality that good things only happen to others. Satan steals our joy, kills our hope, and destroys our potential in an attempt to abort God's plan for us. Thankfully, this is not where the story ends! With our cooperation and through faith and trust in Him, Jesus is more than able to help us become the person we've been created to be.

God desires that we live up to our full potential, overcoming all the obstacles that get in the way of His plan, purpose and destiny for our lives. There are many Old Testament stories of battles fought and won against the odds when God's people followed His plan and strategy in absolute obedience (read the book of Joshua). Who would have thought that marching around a city could bring its walls crumbling down? Or as in the story of David and Goliath, that a single stone would solve the Giant problem? Kingdom strategies seldom make sense to the natural mind.

Through victimization we have been lied to and have learned to expect the worst.

There are also stories of great defeat when people did things their own way, according to what they believed. Just as He did with David and Joshua, God wants to give us the kingdom keys, the biblical principles that show us how to overcome every battle we face. He begins by showing us how to win the battle in our minds.

Our self-image has been formed partly by messages we received through the words and actions of significant people in our lives. Like a computer, we put out what has been programmed into our hearts and minds through our own experiences and interactions. If experience has told us we are worthless, stupid, unlovable, and will never amount to anything, it's obvious we're in need of re-programming because this is completely contrary to what God says about us!

We can, here and now, decide to take responsibility for re-programming our beliefs. We can choose to renew our minds according to what God says about us. In fact God commands us to be transformed by renewing our minds with His Word:

> Do not conform any longer to the pattern of this world, but be transformed by the renewing of your mind. Then you will be able to test and approve what God's will is – His good, perfect and pleasing will (Rom. 12:2 NIV).

No one can stop us from making that decision, nor can anyone force us to make it. It is entirely, completely, 100% up to us. No matter how negative the environment we live or work in, we can allow God to change our beliefs in the midst of it. As we begin to grow in faith, it will become easier to disagree with the old messages and labels we have accepted in the past. It will become easier to stay away from other sources of negative information, such as news or television shows that promote discouragement and depression, or people who drag us down. We change our self-concept in part by changing our influences. Biblical truth should be our greatest influence if we truly desire to be free. Jesus tells us that His followers who *"abide in [His] Word will know the truth, and the truth will set [them] free"* (John 8:32 NKJV).

We can, here and now, decide to take responsibility for re-programming our beliefs.

If this sounds too simple, that's because it is! Learning God's truth is a choice. The difficult part is that it requires our commitment, cooperation and diligence on a daily basis to make it happen. Submitting to God in prayer regardless of how we feel is vital. Our feelings are the worst thing to follow when we want real change. The more broken we are on the inside, the more we need truth to restore us.

Think of it as having come to the end of a long illness and the body is in a weakened state. We have choices to make regarding the speed and effectiveness of our recovery; if we do everything the doctor, nutritionist, and physiotherapist recommend we have the greatest chance of a complete and speedy recovery. It is the same with our mind, will, and emotions. The more truth we allow in, the more effective the recovery will be.

> **Our feelings are the worst thing to follow when we want real change.**

Now imagine that once we begin to experience the positive effects of acting on the doctor's advice we decide to do further research. A look into the benefits of health foods, vitamin supplements and weight training may convince us that these measures will further enhance the effectiveness of our recovery. The same is true about the power of God's Word! It heals and restores our spiritual, emotional and physical strength by renewing our minds. We choose how much we will "feed" ourselves each day, and how active we will be in living out our transformed beliefs.

While it is true that we cannot hurry God, it is also true that in many cases we are probably holding Him up. The Hebrew slaves wandered in the desert for forty years because they never learned to fully trust God's promises. Their minds remained conformed to the pattern of the world they'd lived in. Their beliefs remained stuck in the slave mindsets of their old life in Egypt, even though God had freed their bodies with Moses' help years before. Their beliefs kept them bound to their worldly belief system rather than to God's kingdom belief system.

God is waiting patiently for us to come into line with His will for us, first transforming our minds so that we can know what His will for us is. Though God puts no requirement on how much time we should spend in His Word or in communication with Him, the benefits we'll see are in direct proportion to the time and trust we give Him.

It is the same with our bodies. If we know that it takes three one-hour sessions a week at the gym to reach a reasonable level of fitness, we are free to set up our schedule that way. We also have the choice to work out two hours each time or five times a week, knowing it will increase the results.

Many of us believe that having a devotional time every morning, prayers at meals and before bed, plus church on Sunday is enough to keep God happy. In reality, God wants us to do these things for our benefit. It is in these times that He can communicate His truth and direction to us. He takes joy in knowing we are walking in obedience and wanting to communicate with Him. But He also knows that the more time we spend in His Word and in prayer, the more victory we will experience in our lives and the more positive impact we will have on others.

> **Some will argue that life is already too busy... the truth is, if we are serious about changing, we will find the time.**

Some will argue that life is already too busy; there just isn't enough time to take on more. This is a typical victim response. The truth is if we are serious about changing, we will find the time. We will turn off the television and talk less on the phone. Instead of listening to the car radio we will stock up on teaching or the Bible on CD. We'll stop reading meaningless books and magazines, and begin reading testimonies of people who have walked the path we are on and overcame their struggles. We will begin to pray for the frustrating people in our lives instead of complaining about them. We'll join a group where we can be built up, encouraged, and held accountable, while we do the same for others. Scary as all this may sound, it is what real commitment to change looks like. If we are serious about leaving our victim mentality in the dust, we will begin to implement some of these changes. Our circumstances cannot keep us captive unless we believe they are in control!

God wants us to be free of everything that is sucking up our time and energy, so ask Him to show you what is keeping you from devoting yourself to Him. (Even if you did this after reading the introduction, there may be more.) We probably won't like what God shows us because these habits give us comfort and pleasure. If that

> **We probably won't like what God shows us because these habits give us comfort and pleasure.**

weren't true we wouldn't keep them up. We need His help to give them up. Look at where they have gotten us so far: unmotivated, overweight, suffering from poor self-image, weak, cultivating superficial relationships with God and others, broke, bitter and resentful. Remember, it is considered insanity to keep doing the same things we've always done and expect a different result.

Let's look at what could happen to our quality of life if we changed only one current influence. Let's say for example that we decide to turn off the TV for one week. What should we expect to have happen to us? We may feel a bit out of touch at work or school, but so what? People thrive on talking about this stuff and sooner or later they'll catch us up on anything that's important.

We may also experience some boredom in the evenings – perhaps we'll get bored enough to play with our kids or take a walk with our spouse. We may even begin to call our mothers more often! Worse still we could end up clearing out the garage/basement/closet. After all, we've only put that off for the last six months! Our kids or spouse may even help and we'll finally discover the secret to quality time: shared experiences and opportunities to talk about something other than homework or the rising cost of gas. Did I mention that we'll also find out where all our time really goes?

Some other potentially "hazardous" side effects that come to mind might include getting to bed earlier and feeling more energetic during waking hours. We may even begin to talk to God at weird unscheduled times, and because there is no background noise, we may actually hear His still small voice giving us the direction we need to live a successful and peaceful life. The list could go on and on but I think by now we should have grasped the general idea. When we change our influences, it affects other things.

Through this process God will begin to show us things about ourselves that we may not be too excited about. He will show us how our pride has blinded us from seeing our own shortcomings. He will fine-tune our attitudes, and if we respond with repentance, we will experience great freedom from the old habits and mindsets that have become strongholds in our lives. We will cease to be the centre of our own world, and become more aware of the needs around us. I know this because it is what God had to do with me.

> *"Now all glory to God, who is able, through his mighty power at work within us, to accomplish infinitely more than we might ask or think."*
>
> *Ephesians 3:20 NLT*

Who or what are you currently allowing to influence and set limitations on your life?

Chapter 6

PERCEPTIONS

*So will I choose their delusions, and bring their fears
on them; because, when I called, no one answered; when
I spoke they did not hear.*

ISAIAH 66:4 NKJV

How we view situations, circumstances and people is the result of the perceptions we have developed over our lifetime. This explains why several people can witness the same incident, yet interpret it very differently. The same situation can cause one person extreme anxiety, while another takes it in stride. Job interviews, public speaking, the first day at school, and taking a test can all produce different reactions in different people.

Imagine your view of things as if you are looking through coloured lenses. Our experiences and influences have produced filters in our minds through which our thoughts and observations must pass. Our minds decide what we are seeing or hearing and whether we should accept it as truth or not. When our perceptions are incorrect, we receive lies as if they are truth. In the same way we may reject truth as lies.

At their root, our perceptions are based in either faith or fear; we react to circumstances out of one or the other.

> **Our experiences and influences have produced filters in our minds through which our thoughts and observations must pass.**

Situations that are not even threatening can appear so if our filters are clogged or coloured with faulty beliefs. This will cause us to respond to situations in ways that eventually cause our fears to become a reality. We all have fears that need to be replaced by faith in God.

Do you fear any of the following?

- losing your job
- never getting married
- getting sick
- losing a loved one
- growing old
- being betrayed
- being lonely
- being penniless
- death
- rejection
- change

Whether we realize it or not, our fears in any of these areas can actually lead us to make choices that cause them to happen. Fear of losing a job, a spouse or friends may cause us to act in compromising ways. We may make poor choices in an attempt to please and impress people so we won't get fired, rejected or abandoned. Ultimately there will always be someone who will come along and do it better, look better, be smarter or be more willing to compromise standards! Choosing to act out of fear is an open door to Satan because it removes you from the protection and provision that only comes through faith in God.

A fear-filled person typically adopts a victim mentality and becomes easy to manipulate and control. A faith-filled person in the same situation will garner respect because of their integrity and uncompromising behaviour. Even if they lose in a physical sense they will gain in the spiritual. They may be shaken but will not fall apart because their faith in God gives them the assurance of His provision and protection. Their motives are completely different because their trust is in God. Therefore they cannot be controlled or manipulated or made to feel powerless. For example, if both the fearful and the faith-filled person lost their jobs, their reactions would be very different. One would be devastated, lost and confused, while the other would be challenged but still hopeful and confident of what God has for them in the future.

Choosing to act out of fear is an open door to Satan because it removes you from the protection and provision that only comes through faith in God.

Fear of failure leads to desperation. We all know people who are desperately afraid of never getting married. Their fears can drive them several different ways, none leading to the results they desire. Each failed relationship leaves them more disillusioned and depressed. Desperation is not on anyone's list of attractive qualities in a mate. It does, however, make a person easy prey for someone with impure motives.

When we really believe God has good plans for our lives and wants us to have the desires of our hearts, we will allow Him to line up our desires with His. In relation to the example mentioned above, we will trust Him and stop using flattery, charm, manipulation or seduction to snag a mate. When we fish with the wrong bait, we may just catch a shark! Confessing our fears and finding truth will change our perceptions of God, ourselves and others.

> *"You're blessed when you get your inside world—your mind and heart—put right. Then you can see God in the outside world."*

> *Matthew 5:8 NIV*

The closer we get to seeing things God's way, the clearer and truer our perceptions become.

Chapter 7

EXPERIENCES

For most of my life I figured I was pretty smart. I had lots of answers even when no one was asking any questions. Then there came a time when I could no longer come up with the answers I needed.

I had become a Christian several months after moving to Canada. I tried hard to be a good Christian because I was convinced life would be better if I did. I learned quickly how to dress, walk and talk like other Christians. I observed how some Christian women seemed to be fulfilled by baking from scratch, canning pears, and tending elaborate vegetable gardens. I tried that too, but it just didn't work for me. It took a few guilt-ridden years of trying to fit that mold before I discovered that God had a unique purpose for each one of His children. It didn't matter to Him one bit if I didn't grow my own tomatoes! However there were things I did need to

> **I observed how some Christian women seemed to be fulfilled by baking from scratch, canning pears, and tending elaborate vegetable gardens.**

learn if I was to get out of the frustrating cycle I'd been stuck in.

I would love to be able to tell you I learned the principles and keys in this book solely by studying Scripture, but that would not be true. I have been guilty of pretty much all of the wrong beliefs and attitudes I discuss throughout these chapters. If I hadn't opened my heart and mind to the possibility that the things I didn't like about my life weren't always someone else's fault I would still be fighting for my right to be right instead of writing this book. I had plenty of legitimate reasons to be angry.

I had emigrated from Ireland to Canada with my four-month-old baby, bowing to the pressure of a persistent husband who, after three years of urging had finally convinced me this was best for us. In the process I sacrificed family relationships, friendships, and all the comforts that familiarity brings. I had been persuaded to believe that this would be the dream life. The bitterness came as the dream quickly crumbled, and I realized some truths about the illusion I had been living. The main cause of my confusion and disillusionment in the marriage surfaced for the first time when I discovered my husband's adulterous ways.

> **The bitterness came as the dream quickly crumbled, and I realized some truths about the illusion I had been living.**

We'd been living in Canada for four years when the problems in our marriage increased dramatically. A friend had moved into our basement apartment some months earlier after her marriage had failed – the result of an affair she'd had with her best friend's husband. I know you are asking yourself what on earth I was thinking! At the time it seemed to be a practical solution for both parties, financially beneficial to us and practically beneficial to her. Keep in mind that at this point I had never realized my husband had problems in this area.

Anyhow, after I'd learned about the affair and upon the advice and encouragement of this "friend", I returned to Ireland with my children, believing that my marriage was past saving. I was sad about how things had gone, but glad to be able to go back to the support I knew the children and I would have there.

I hadn't been back long when I learned that the real reason she had been so encouraging and he so indifferent was that they had been having an affair for many months. I also began to learn that this was not the first time he'd strayed. It seemed that my separation from him finally gave people the freedom to tell me what they'd been hesitant to before. I began to realize just what a deluded life I had been living. With this reality to deal with I began to settle in, glad to have left the worst behind me back in Canada.

My relief was short-lived; the next blow came quickly! I went to see a lawyer to ensure that things were settled legally, but it turned out that different laws applied because it was an international situation. After meeting with an attorney I was left with no more delusions about my situation. She said that under the Geneva Convention my children could be

I pondered and meditated on my sorry state daily, always having others to sympathize and support me, agreeing that I was indeed a victim.

summoned back to Canada at any time on my ex-husband's whim, or if they went to visit him he could just keep them there. She had no doubt my ex was well aware of his rights considering he was in law enforcement. I asked for my options, only to be told there weren't any. Her only advice was "go back and make it work." So I did.

My husband had been busy in my absence playing the role of the broken-hearted abandoned husband. He and his mistress had been working hard at denying their affair. Fortunately there was no way they could continue to defend their innocence and continue living under the same

63

roof once I showed that I was willing to come back and try again.

We remained together for several years until the lying and abuse made it impossible to stay in what had become an increasingly hurtful, dysfunctional, unstable relationship. So after twelve years of marriage I left for the last time with my now three children ages seven, three and two years old, seeking refuge in a women's shelter.

I could give you many more details that would make you feel really sorry for me, but there would be no point. My husband's sins of cheating and lying were the big ones, so my anger and disrespect seemed insignificant in comparison. They seemed so small; they were easily hidden, even from me. It is sufficient to say that years of legal wrangling and battles over money and children followed,

> **The result of not taking responsibility for our own dysfunctions means our children will have to deal with some consequences we, as parents, could have prevented.**

allowing for many opportunities for both sides to be bitter, angry and resentful. For a long time I took every one of those opportunities. I pondered and meditated on my sorry state daily, always having others to sympathize and support me, agreeing that I was indeed a victim, no matter which way I looked at it. Life was out of my control, and nothing could change until my ex did, or so I thought.

While I chose to focus on what had been done to me, life just kept passing me by. I must have missed countless opportunities to enjoy life more. Keeping company with negativity, bitterness and unforgiveness just doesn't add up to a fun time, not to mention the impact it has on those closest to you, namely your children.

My bitterness caused me to become controlling (I needed to protect them from that terrible person and all his lies). It took me years to see this. In my mind I really was protecting them. Controlling your children comes with a price. In my case it resulted in periods of estrangement from two of my children. The result of not taking responsibility for our own dysfunctions means our children will have to deal with some consequences we, as parents, could have prevented. While I'm not happy that any of this had to happen, I know God takes the most miserable of our failures and supernaturally turns things around in ways we cannot imagine.

So in short what I'm saying is this: by choosing to do things God's way – by taking responsibility for our own lives and messes instead of wasting time in blaming and bitterness – we can avoid the pain and consequences that our wrong attitudes will bring. I had to begin by just being open to the possibility that I was somehow in the wrong. If you are serious about change you'll need to start there too.

> *"And we know that God causes everything to work together for the good of those who love God and are called according to his purpose for them."*
>
> *Romans 8:28 NLT*

It is never too late to give your past mistakes to God. Just trust Him and do things His way from now on, He can make a ministry out of your mess!

Part 2

EXPOSING THE HEART

The heart is hopelessly dark and deceitful, a
puzzle no one can figure out.
But I, God, search the heart and examine the
mind.
I get to the heart of the human.
I get to the root of things.
I treat them as they really are, not as they
pretend to be.
Jeremiah 17:9-10 MSG

Chapter 8

MOTIVES

*All the ways of a man are pure in his own eyes, but the
Lord weighs the spirits (the thoughts and intents of the
heart.)*

PROVERBS 16:2 AMP

God seems to be more concerned about the condition
of our hearts than anything else. He knows that everything
about us that is visible only reflects what is in our hearts;
our heart is the very core of who we are. It is at the center
of all we do.

God tells us that we are deceived by our own hearts.
In other words, we lie to ourselves about what's really in
there. But God cannot be fooled. He knows exactly what
our motives are, and treats us according to them, not
according to the behaviour we may put on display.

Scripture also tells us that above everything else we
should guard our hearts because whatever we allow to get
in there will determine the course of our life (Prov. 4:23
NLT).

So how are we to do that? In the first part of this book we discussed how influences and experiences impact what we believe and how we think and act. Our hearts are filled with knowledge and information that enters through our ears and eyes. This information is filtered through our minds before it is deposited in our hearts. Our filters decide what gets through. Not all random

Until we are honest about what really motivates us and repent of it, we will not fully submit to God.

thoughts make it into our heart, but those we give significance to and meditate on will enter into our hearts and help shape our perceptions of life, God, and our own self-image. This is why the changes that we attempt to make by just trying to think differently are not long-lasting. It's the thinking and believing at the heart level that needs to be transformed in order for change to be permanent. That means getting the truth through the mind and into the heart. Proverbs 23:7 tells us that as we think in our heart, so we are.

We become what we believe in our hearts, not just in our minds. Our mind is just the starting place for beliefs to be formed. We are constantly evaluating new information deciding what to accept and reject. When we have a good day our faith and confidence rises. If it's a bad day,

Having wrong attitudes, pretending they don't exist and then trying to get away with them is like eating a tub of ice cream daily and hoping it won't eventually show up on your thighs.

our confidence falls and fear settles in. The battle for our lives is fought in our thought life, which is why God cautions us to take our thoughts captive at that level. Once thoughts make it into our hearts they will define who we are and proceed to guide and direct our decisions and choices about the issues of life, even when they are wrong.

The unregenerate heart is always self seeking; it believes it has to find ways to have needs met because it does not believe God can be trusted to do this. Our hearts must be changed so we can willingly obey God. Until we are honest about what really motivates us and repent of it, we will not fully submit to God. When we make choices out of our selfish motives we may not realize that we are ultimately choosing against God and His will for us.

God makes it clear that even we cannot understand what's in our hearts — what the true motives are behind everything we do. The Bible tells us that our heart is naturally wicked and therefore contaminates our life and character.

> *The heart is deceitful above all things, and it is exceedingly perverse and corrupt and severely, mortally sick! Who can know it [perceive, understand, be acquainted with his own heart and mind]? I the Lord search the mind, I try the heart, even to give to every man according to his ways, according to the fruit of his doings (Jer. 17:9-10 AMP).*

I don't know about you, but I'm pretty sure I don't want to harvest the fruit of some of my own doings! Having wrong attitudes, pretending they don't exist, and then trying to get away with them is like eating a tub of ice cream daily and hoping it won't eventually show up on your thighs. It's going to happen! We cannot hide the evil that is stored in our hearts; it is going to show up, one way or another.

Our hidden motives can be revealed through the things we seek after with our natural abilities. Among other things, wrong motives may cause us to seek after control, pleasure, significance, power, respect, admiration, freedom, comfort, peace, happiness, meaning, success and love in the wrong way.

The Word of God is the only thing that can cut through all the deception that keeps us stuck in sin and acting with wrong heart motives. Its ability to expose true motives is powerfully revealed in the following verse from Hebrews:

> *For the Word that God speaks is alive and full of power [making it active, operative, energizing, and effective]; it is sharper than any two-edged sword, penetrating to the dividing line of the breath of life (soul) and [the immortal] spirit, and of joints and marrow [of the deepest parts of our nature], exposing and sifting and analyzing and judging the very thoughts and purposes of the heart (Heb 4:12 AMP).*

If we allow God to search our hearts and expose our true motives so we can deal with them properly, we will become useful instruments for His kingdom and fulfill our destiny. If we are convinced that our needs for the things we desire will not be met by God, we will do all we can to meet those needs through other means. We will employ

If we are convinced that our needs for the things we desire will not be met by God, we will do all we can to meet those needs through other means.

methods such as control, manipulation, coercion and intimidation to get what we want. In the end, these tactics will have the opposite effect, driving away the people we love and care about most.

On the other hand, if we truly believe that God wants to meet these needs, then we will do what it takes to grow in faith, let go of all these methods and trust Him to do so. Behind every motive is either fear (worrying that our need won't be met unless we do something) or faith (believing not only that God *can* but that He really *wants* to do it for us). When we are motivated by fear rather than faith it will cause us to move in the wrong direction, right out of the will of God. Motives change once we are convinced of God's desire to be good to us, and can trust that His way of doing things will always have the best outcome in every situation.

The Apostle Paul talks about right and wrong motives in his letter to the Philippians. He writes:

> *Do nothing from factional motives [through contentiousness, strife, selfishness, or for unworthy ends] or prompted by conceit and empty arrogance. Instead, in the true spirit of humility (lowliness of mind) let each regard the others as better than and superior to himself [thinking more highly of one another than you do of yourselves] (Phil. 2:3 AMP).*

Self-preservation and trying to satisfy our own needs and desires without God is behind our wrong motives. These manifest themselves in many different ways, some of which we will expose in the next chapters.

Recognize that there are generally two reasons for doing what you do:

1. The good explanation you give others (the one that brings personal benefit to you).
2. The true reason which you keep hidden.
3. It would be good to admit to yourself that this is true so you can proceed with an open heart, ready to allow the truth to change you and keep your motives in check.

> *"A man's own folly ruins his life, yet his heart rages against the LORD."*
>
> Proverbs 19:3 NIV

Don't continue to live life on your own terms, and then blame God when it goes wrong.

Chapter 9

FORGIVENESS

Father forgive them, for they do not know what they do.
LUKE 23:34 NKJV

Forgiveness is difficult to extend until we recognize how much we ourselves need it. The reality is, every one of us needs to be forgiven for something we've done to hurt another. There isn't a single person who doesn't have a story of hurt or pain that has been inflicted by another. While there are vast differences in individual circumstances and suffering, each of us owe it to ourselves and those we care about to deal with the hurt in a way that will minimize its impact on our lives and relationships.

Just as we ourselves can be insensitive to the hurt we may have caused others, we at some point have to accept that the people who have hurt us may not have fully understood the lasting impact of their words and actions on us either. Some maybe did not realize that the wounds and scars would remain long after the event, and that they would alter the course that our life was meant to take. Others may have known, but just didn't care.

Forgiving people does not mean we have to rationalize or excuse their wrong behaviour. Sin is in the world and suffering is the consequence of things not being done the way God intended. Forgiveness does not ask us to deny what was done to us or its impact on us. Rather, it is for the benefit of the wounded party (us) so that we do not continue to live with the consequences of the hurt or the subsequent bitterness and unforgiveness.

Fundamentally, there is little hope of us reaching our full potential and living abundantly unless the issue of forgiveness is properly dealt with. Unforgiveness is a toxic emotion that will poison every aspect of our lives. Justifying our choice to remain bitter and withhold forgiveness will keep us stuck in the past, and tied emotionally to the perpetrator.

We reason that if we don't take our own revenge by telling others about what's been done to us and continue to hate those who have wronged us, they will escape without consequence. The truth about forgiveness is that you don't have to *feel* like doing it. If you wait for that to happen it probably won't. Contrary to popular opinion, time alone won't make those feelings disappear either. It is your choice to hold on to them that keeps them alive. Forgiveness is a choice, not a feeling. We must do what we know is right. The people who have hurt us may never qualify for our forgiveness; it is a choice we make in obedience to God. They will not experience the full benefit of our forgiving them unless they come asking for it.

> **Unforgiveness is a toxic emotion that will poison every aspect of our lives.**

The harsh reality is that forgiveness can't erase all the consequences of the person's wrong actions against you. Adultery cannot be reversed, virginity cannot be restored after rape, and the person may never return what they stole from you. Forgiving does not mean that you have to condone, overlook, make excuses for, tolerate, or wipe injustice from your memory. What forgiveness *can* do is stop the caustic forces of bitterness from continuing to destroy your life.

Forgiveness does not always mean reconciliation, but we must choose to stop bringing up the offense or replaying it in our minds if we want to heal from the pain those memories bring.

Refusing to forgive carries the past into your today and tomorrow. Like driving a car forward while looking in the rear view mirror, it won't take long before you experience disaster. Real life change is impossible without it; spiritual growth and emotional healing is unattainable without it. This alone should compel us to take forgiveness very seriously.

Real forgiveness means letting go of destructive emotions, negative patterns of thinking, and bitter attitudes that will eventually damage our relationships. It also means having faith that God will be our defender and vindicator. For a time we will have to repeatedly - perhaps daily - affirm our decision to forgive until we have victory.

> **What forgiveness *can* do is stop the caustic forces of bitterness from continuing to destroy your life.**

Eventually we will be amazed at the freedom and release we feel. The memories do not disappear, but if we consistently remind ourselves that we've already forgiven, we will find that it no longer has the power to hurt us.

My own experience of successful forgiving has been that I can easily remember what was done to me, but because there is no longer any anger attached to the memory, I can tell the story as if it happened to someone else. The forgiving process heals the pain associated with the experience.

Jesus had some very uncomfortable things to say about forgiveness. He knew the outcome of unforgiveness, and made it clear that it's not a good option for anyone. His stance on forgiveness is unmistakable: *"For if you forgive men when they sin against you, your Heavenly Father will also forgive you. But if you do not forgive men their sins, your Father will not forgive your sins"* (Matt. 6:14-15 NIV). I don't like this verse any more than you do. As much as I'd like to ignore it or find some theological explanation that provides an exemption clause, I can assure you that none exists. I do believe that when we do things God's way just because He says so; He will turn things around for our good. Our welfare is His concern. When He tells us to do something a certain way, it's always for our good, even when it doesn't make sense to the natural mind.

The story of Joseph (Genesis chapters 37 - 45) gives an example which shows that faith and forgiveness form the most powerful combination for victorious living. First, Joseph is sold into slavery by his older brothers, and then is falsely accused of trying to seduce his master's wife. He spends years in prison for a crime he'd never committed. He could understandably have justified withholding forgiveness from his brothers, yet he chose to believe and obey God regardless of his circumstances. God restored Joseph beyond his wildest dreams to the second highest position in the land! Joseph consistently made the right choices and kept his attitude right because he knew nothing was as important as doing things God's way. For Joseph forgiveness clearly was not optional, he'd made it his lifestyle. God's plan and purpose won out every time that Joseph chose not to get angry, not to complain, not to give up, and not to question

When we forgive, we clear away obstacles and limitations in our thinking which could potentially hinder our progress.

When we forgive, we clear away obstacles and limitations in our thinking which could potentially hinder our progress. We avoid the frustration of spending years wondering what went wrong. Instead, we trust God to show us what we need to know when we need to know it. The people and circumstances that caused the pain can no longer distract us from our God-given destiny. Furthermore, the energy that used to be consumed by bitterness, anger, and hatred can instead be used in more positive ways. We no longer need to be suspicious or try to settle the score. God will do whatever needs to be done when we get out of His way. Our relationships will improve because we no longer impose our negativity on those around us. We trust God to protect us, and we cease from our self-protective behaviors. God is our protector; He is our vindicator. We do our part, which is to forgive those who have hurt us, and we trust and allow God to do His.

Again, your choice to forgive sets YOU free; the only difference it may make to the forgiven person is that they no longer have to deal with any negativity you've been displaying towards them. THEY will not be freed from the consequences of their actions until they take full responsibility and repent.

> *"Therefore, I tell you, her many sins have been forgiven—for she loved much. But he who has been forgiven little loves little."*
>
> *Luke 7:47 NIV*

Deal with your unforgiveness before it deals with you.

Chapter 10

CONFESSION & REPENTANCE

*Confess your sins to each other and pray for each other so
that you may be healed. The earnest prayer of a
righteous person has great power and produces wonderful
results.*

JAMES 5:16 NLT

God has given us confession and repentance as no-fail ways of dealing with our sinful attitudes and anything else that keeps us from experiencing His best. It's impossible to fully repent unless we first acknowledge our own sin. Repentance means turning away from our sin and changing our behaviour. It was repentance that John the Baptizer emphasized as he prepared the people of Israel for their Messiah. We read of His challenge to, *"repent (think differently; change your mind, regretting your sins and changing your conduct), for the kingdom of heaven is at hand"* (Matt. 3:1-2 AMP).

We've already touched on the fact that seeing other people's sin is easy compared to seeing our own. But it's when we see and acknowledge our own sins that kingdom principles become easier to understand. Unconfessed sin will stand in the way of our relationship with God. It will eventually negatively affect every area of life if we keep trying to hide it. Often we can't see the connection between our problems and the hidden sin behind them because we've been hiding and denying it for so long.

There is only one thing that any of us can contribute to our own salvation and that is repentance. When we repent, we are admitting that we've done wrong and need help. Repentance is the first step in realizing our need for a relationship with Jesus. Ongoing repentance is necessary if we want to live a changed life, because it is the result of recognizing that there are things we need to change. We gain understanding of how to live righteously and deal with sin when we examine our hearts, take responsibility for what we find wrong and then confess and repent of it.

> **Unconfessed sin will stand in the way of our relationship with God. It will eventually negatively affect every area of life if we keep trying to hide it.**

Harbouring sin gets in the way of our communication with God. The Psalmist writes, *"If I regard iniquity in my heart the Lord will not hear me"* (Psalm 66:18 AMP). Is the Lord hearing your prayers, or is unconfessed sin getting in the way?

Repenting of our sin and accepting Jesus as Lord and Savior is the only way to enter the Kingdom of God. However, the benefits of repentance go beyond this. Every time we are convicted of sin and truly repent, we experience more of God's kingdom reality in our lives; more of His mercy, His forgiveness and His power. True repentance empties us of ourselves and makes room for the Holy Spirit to fill us with God's knowledge and wisdom, enabling us to successfully live out our purpose and enjoy His blessings, as we read in Psalm 32:

"Blessed (happy, fortunate, to be envied) is the man to whom the Lord imputes no iniquity and in whose spirit there is no deceit" (Psalm 32:2 AMP).

Satan uses fear to convince us to hide our sin because he knows the blessings that come from repentance. The last thing he wants is for us to experience true freedom. His objective is to destroy us by keeping us blinded by guilt and fear, ineffective for God and unaware of the purpose of God's kindness which, as Paul

> **Underestimating God's goodness can keep us from experiencing the freedom, blessing and happiness that result from repentance.**

says to the Romans, is to lead us to repentance: *"Are you unmindful or actually ignorant [of the fact] that God's kindness is intended to lead you to repent (to change your mind and inner man to accept God's will)?"* (Rom. 2:4 AMP).

Underestimating God's goodness can keep us from experiencing the freedom, blessing and happiness that result from repentance. The Psalmist shares of God's immediate response to his heartfelt repentance:

> *I acknowledged my sin to You, and my iniquity I did not hide. I said, I will confess my transgressions to the Lord [continually unfolding the past till all is told] - then You [instantly] forgave me the guilt and iniquity of my sin (Psalm 32:5 AMP).*

Don't let fear or shame of past mistakes and wrong choices keep you in hiding. Make the most of every opportunity these chapters present to get honest with yourself and God. You can experience His instant forgiveness as you *"unfold your past before Him until all is told"* (Psalm 32:5). He wants to turn your life around, so whatever He brings to your mind as you read, confess it, repent of it and you will become free!

> "Bring forth fruit that is consistent with repentance [let your lives prove your change of heart]."
>
> Matthew 3:8 AMP

The evidence of true repentance is a changed life.

Chapter 11

DESIRES

Trust in the Lord and do good. Then you will live safely in the land and prosper. Take delight in the Lord, and he will give you your heart's desires.

PSALM 37:3-4 NLT

Our heart will desire whatever it believes will make us happy. Our desires are forces that drive our lives towards either good or evil, depending on how we exercise our will. God wants us to have the desires of our hearts, but not until He knows that our desires are consistent with His. He knows that some of the things we crave will eventually destroy us if we get them. Sometimes we are unable to recognize the desires that could bring us harm because we are not in tune with God's plans and are unaware of our own true motives. God will never support selfish choices because He knows they will take us on a path of pain and failure, but He will make sure our desires are satisfied completely if we will trust Him and do things His way.

People who are driven by selfish desires will seek satisfaction in any way they can, but ultimately they (and those around them) will pay the price for their selfishness. In order to have illegitimate desires met, some will manipulate, control, deceive, abuse and violate without any regard for another's well being. The following verses clearly illustrate some results of pursuing our desires selfishly:

> *What is causing the quarrels and fights among you? Don't they come from the evil desires at war within you? You want what you don't have, so you scheme and kill to get it. You are jealous of what others have, but you can't get it, so you fight and wage war to take it away from them. Yet you don't have what you want because you don't ask God for it. And even when you ask, you don't get it because your motives are all wrong—you want only what will give you pleasure* (James 4: 1-3 NLT).

Most of what we crave for in life – even money, sex and power – stems from legitimate God-given desires. He will meet these desires in ways that will benefit those involved, but only if we are willing to do it His way. Problems arise when we begin to look to other sources because we do not trust God to meet and satisfy these desires. Drugs, alcohol, food, praise and wrong attention can actually dampen our desire for a relationship with God and the good things He would have us find satisfaction in. These are all ways by which we attempt to satisfy our desires without dependence on God.

Meeting our needs in our way and in our own power reveals that we are lacking faith in His desire to meet them. For example, a woman who is desperate for love may settle for being a married man's mistress. Or perhaps we will lie and cheat on our taxes because we don't trust God to provide for us financially. If we continue focusing on wrong desires it will cause us to make one compromising decision after another. The desires we focus on will ultimately consume our lives. When knowing God and seeking His kingdom become the primary desire of our hearts, every other desire will be kept in balance. In his letter to the Romans the Apostle Paul contrasts the unholy "flesh-based" life with the Spirit-filled one:

> **If, we continue focusing on wrong desires it will cause us to make one compromising decision after another.**

> *For those who are according to the flesh and are controlled by its unholy desires set their minds on and pursue those things which gratify the flesh, but those who are according to the Spirit and are controlled by the desires of the Spirit set their minds on and seek those things which gratify the [Holy] Spirit (Rom. 8:5 AMP).*

The very first sin was a result of Adam and Eve believing that God was withholding good things from them (Genesis 2:17, 3:1-6). God never wanted them to eat from the Tree of Knowledge of good and evil for very good reason.

God set boundaries for Adam and Eve because He did not want them to experience the "knowledge" of hate, murder, divorce, death, physical pain, poverty, or sexual abuse, all the pain that "knowing" sin would bring with it. Yet they made the choice to entertain evil, letting Satan deceive them against the true knowledge God had given them - the knowledge of God and His goodness. Sin has challenged our knowledge of God ever since. How often do we say things like "I know I shouldn't, but...?" Sin always leads to destruction.

Today we fall into the same trap when, even as believers, we look for worldly answers to life's problems. Would we really look outside of God's Word if we truly believed the satisfaction we desire were to be found there? The consequences of demanding God meet our needs our way and in our time will be more than we want to experience! He will let us have what we want, but at what cost? When we wander out of God's perfect plan and will, we will never find His solutions, or the happiness and success He has in store for us. Like the Hebrew slaves in the desert, He may give us what we insist on having, but we will also have to deal with the consequences.

> **He may give us what we insist on having, but we will also have to deal with the consequences.**

The Hebrews experienced this principle in spades as they wandered around the desert. The Psalmist, writing about the experience of his ancestors, warns the people of Israel about the folly of their fathers, who "craved intensely in the wilderness" and "tempted God" with their requests. In verse 15 he warns, *"And He gave them their request, but sent leanness into their souls and [thinned their numbers by] disease and death"* (Psalm 106:14-15 AMP).

The most shocking thing is that God will let us have what we want if we insist on it, even if it kills us! It's worth noting we live in a world where people don't seek after or follow God's direction as they should, but somehow still feel justified in blaming Him when things go wrong as a result of what they themselves have chosen to do.

In contrast, look at what happens when we allow God to satisfy our desires His way. Not only are our desires satisfied, but He saves us from destructive paths. It seems He will even reverse the aging process as a bonus! The following verses reflect just how much God desires to bless us:

> *Bless (affectionately, gratefully praise) the Lord, O my soul, and forget not [one of] all His benefits; Who forgives [every one of] all your iniquities, Who heals [each one of] all your diseases, Who redeems your life*

*from the pit and corruption, Who beautifies, dignifies,
and crowns you with lovingkindness and tender mercy;
Who satisfies your mouth [your necessity and desire at
your personal age and situation] with good so that
your youth, renewed, is like the eagle's [strong,
overcoming, soaring]!*

Psalm 103:2-5 AMP

Now *that* is satisfaction with a side benefit package!
Who wouldn't want it? There is only one way to have
our true desires satisfied: His way. There is no more
room for compromise.

Chapter 12

EXPECTATIONS

*Be strong and let your heart take courage, all you who
wait for and hope for and expect the Lord!*

PSALM 31:24 AMP

Previous life experience has conditioned us to expect
certain things. We live daily with these expectations without
even being aware of them. As if this wasn't complicated
enough, we are also subconsciously trying to live according
to others' expectations of us.

Expectations are like unspoken demands. The right
kinds of expectations motivate us to live better, energize us,
and help us achieve our best. Wrong expectations on the
other hand, weigh down the spirit. The burden of wrong
expectations can cause discouragement, a sense of wanting
to give up without trying because the bar is set too high.
They are big-time relationship killers. If we want to have an
abundance of disappointment in our lives we just need to
keep a long list of wrong expectations of ourselves, God,

and everyone we know! Wrong expectations are an unseen pressure that will eventually overwhelm everyone who tries to live up to them. The Bible is full of God's expectations of His people to do great things in His power. It also teaches us some amazing things we can expect from God. The question is, whose expectations are we trying to live up to? Are they God's expectations of us, our own, or someone else's unrealistic expectations?

When people have unhealthy expectations resulting from past unresolved issues, these will eventually be imposed on the wrong people. For instance, you may not have felt secure growing up, so now you depend on your spouse, employer or even the government to provide that sense of security rather than leaning on God.

In relationships, unspoken fears and areas of weakness and deficiency cause us to place burdens of wrong expectation on others. Simply imagine the pressure that fear of abandonment places on relationships. It can lead to control, jealousy, anxiety, insecurity and anger.

Consider any unrealistic expectations you have of others. Think of how it feels when someone tries to guilt us into doing something against our will or better judgment. God shows us that demanding our way leads to contentions. Do your unspoken expectations of others reflect God's ways? If not, they will lead to disappointment, anger and bitterness when they are not met. The expectations we have of others are created by what we believe we are entitled to have from them. In reality we need to let go of any sense of entitlement if we want healthy relationships. God's wants us to live unselfishly knowing that when we do things His way He will take care of all our needs.

> **If we want to have an abundance of disappointment in our lives we just need to keep a long list of wrong expectations of ourselves, God, and everyone we know!**

Another aspect of expectations that we need to deal with are the expectations of a life guided by either fear or faith. Satan continually bombards our minds with negative information, planting seeds of doubt so we'll make fear-based decisions. He sets us up to doubt God and expect the worst. Both faith and fear are forces which are powerful and contagious. We are in control of which one we allow to dominate our expectations of life. Not only does the force we allow to dominate affect us, it also impacts everyone around us.

People set each other up unknowingly to fear situations and expect either the best or worst. We each have the power to influence the people around us to both expect and experience the best life God has to offer, or to live in fear of things constantly going wrong. We must encourage expectations of faith and hope instead of fear and failure. When our expectations line up with God's, we speak words of faith. When we do this we will continually set people up to expect good, especially from God.

Fears are an expectation that bad things will happen. Like faith, they can be passed on from generation to generation. Perhaps one of your parents hated going to the dentist or flying. Their negative reaction may have passed on to you. The most well-meaning parents manage to do this to their children, painting a picture of worst case-scenarios, and then wonder why they have anxiety issues!

I had one misguided mother tell me proudly how she prepared her son for high school. She warned him that there were only three kinds of kids in high school: the bullies, the ones that get bullied and the ones that stand around watching and refuse to do anything about it. Can you even imagine what it was like for this boy in the weeks leading up to the first day of high school? Fear-based predictions limit our experiences and expectations in life, causing some to give up without ever trying. Procrastination and lack of motivation are often the result.

Check your own expectations in every relationship. Allow the Word to give you a new set of expectations according to what God says about you and your future.

> *And therefore the Lord [earnestly] waits [expecting, looking, and longing] to be gracious to you; and therefore He lifts Himself up, that He may have mercy on you and show loving-kindness to you. For the Lord is a God of justice. Blessed (happy, fortunate, to be envied) are all those who [earnestly] wait for Him, who expect and look and long for Him [for His victory, His favor, His love, His peace, His joy, and His matchless, unbroken companionship]!*
>
> Isaiah 30:18 AMP

Your wildest expectations are no match for the things God desires to do in and through you!

Chapter 13

PRIDE & STUBBORNNESS

*{He} is puffed up with pride and stupefied with conceit,
[although he is] woefully ignorant. He has a morbid
fondness for controversy and disputes and strife about
words, which result in (produce) envy and jealousy,
quarrels and dissension, abuse and insults and slander, and
base suspicions.*

1 Timothy 6:4 AMP

Just for a few moments, let's stop kidding ourselves
about having all the answers, and just admit that we actually
have a problem with pride. Only then can we really look
honestly at what life is telling us. The condition of our life
is always telling us something; it may be something we
don't want to hear. The way we experience life reveals what
we really believe and trust in.

We must first admit to ourselves that as humans we
can fail, be wrong, and still be worthy of love and
acceptance. Pride makes us want to hide these sinful parts

of ourselves and pretend they don't exist. But just like Adam and Eve failed to hide their shame from God with their little fig leaves, there is nothing we ourselves can do to conceal pride. Pride puffs us up, makes us vocal, and invites arguments and strife - all things that draw attention. The sin of pride thrives on attention, recognition, and impressing others.

Proud people rely heavily on their strengths, not on God. Proud people can't take advice because listening requires humility, which is the complete opposite of pride.

They also have difficulty receiving the truth of God's Word. Convinced they already know it all, they remain trapped because they will not receive the knowledge needed for their breakthrough. Their arrogance causes them to build higher and higher walls of defense and self-protection to maintain their position of being right. Pride contaminates our motives and is only cured by humility.

> **Proud people can't take advice because listening requires humility, which is the complete opposite of pride.**

What follows is the story of Naaman, a commander of the King of Aram's army who was suffering from leprosy. Having been told of God's prophet Elisha by a servant girl, and encouraged by his king to go to the prophet, he did so. But because he took his pride with him he almost failed to get his healing:

> *So Naaman went with his horses and chariots and waited at the door of Elisha's house. But Elisha sent a messenger out to him with this message: "Go and wash yourself seven times in the Jordan River. Then your skin will be restored, and you will be healed of your leprosy."*

> *But Naaman became angry and stalked away. "I thought he would certainly come out to meet me!" he said. "I expected him to wave his hand over the leprosy*

*and call on the name of the Lord his God and heal
me! Aren't the rivers of Damascus, the Abana and
the Pharpar, better than any of the rivers of Israel?
Why shouldn't I wash in them and be healed?" So
Naaman turned and went away in a rage.*

*But his officers tried to reason with him and said,
"Sir if the prophet had told you to do something very
difficult, wouldn't you have done it? So you should
certainly obey him when he says simply, 'Go and wash
and be cured!' So Naaman went down to the Jordan
River and dipped himself seven times, as the man of
God had instructed him. And his skin became as
healthy as the skin of a young child's, and he was
healed! (2 Kings 5:9-14 NLT).*

Because of his pride Naaman expected his miracle on
his terms, by his standards. This did
not include bath time in the Jordan
river! Not when there were much
nicer rivers back home. Thankfully
he had humble people with him who
could reason with him. If he hadn't
humbled himself you would have been reading a different
story right now!

> **Naman
> expected his
> miracle on his
> terms, by his
> standards.**

Unless we allow God to deal with our pride we'll
never experience His best, and we will eventually be
humbled as a consequence. Satan's pride was his downfall;
it doesn't need to be yours. Jesus' warning to us concerning
pride is clear:

*Whoever exalts himself [with haughtiness and empty
pride] shall be humbled (brought low), and whoever
humbles himself [whoever has a modest opinion of
himself and behaves accordingly] shall be raised to
honor (Matt. 23:12 AMP).*

Pride blinds us from receiving the answers to our problems. It blocks out the insights, knowledge, understanding and wisdom from God's Word that would show us the solutions we need. Pride blinds us to many things, particularly our own foolishness.

One extremely detrimental way that pride manifests itself in our lives is through stubbornness. Stubbornness has quite a few definitions: hard-hearted, obstinate, unteachable, unyielding, or unwilling to change, just to name a few. None of them paint a nice picture. Any one of these attributes will keep us stuck in our problems by blinding us to the real truth about ourselves. Stubbornness renders us inflexible; keeping us trapped in a world of self-delusion. We become oblivious to the fact that it is our own choice to remain closed and ignorant rather than being open to finding the truth we desperately need.

> **Satan's pride was his downfall; it doesn't need to be yours.**

We can easily recognize when we see stubbornness at work in someone else's life. In the same way, others can easily see in us what we refuse to see in ourselves. So it escapes us that we are the major player in the complicated games which define so much of our life. No doubt some may have tried to point out the truth kindly, but because of stubbornness we missed it. Those who've tried harsher methods to make us aware of our problems have been discounted as controlling, crazy or just plain rude and insensitive. The reality is, we are the common denominator in all of our problems. Blinders need to be removed to let us catch a glimpse of what is holding us from the freedom that we want.

Our stubbornness and inability to hear closes the door to the help we really need. For example, a husband comes home to find that his wife has packed up and left him. A note on the kitchen table tells him she's given up hope of him ever changing. He tells people he never saw it coming, never knew she felt that way, and he wonders why she didn't just tell him.

In every case like this I've ever encountered, the cause is very similar. When I ask what kind of things his wife expressed concern about over the years, they'll have a list: she said I drank too much, didn't help enough around the house, spent more time on the computer than with her and the kids, didn't talk to her etc.

The reality is, we are the common denominator in all of our problems.

Even though people hear these comments over and over, it's obvious they haven't really listened, because when someone really listens it will lead to action. In relationships, stubborn people will turn those around them into nags or exasperate them completely! People can only stand not being heard for so long before they give up. James likens the stubborn person to a fool who looks at his face in a mirror, but promptly forgets what he has seen as soon as he walks away. It is of no use to "just listen" to God's Word. You must do what it says. Otherwise you are only fooling yourself (James 1:22-24 NLT). On the other hand, a person who "looks carefully into the perfect law" (God's law of liberty) and does what it says will be blessed by God (James 1:25 NLT).

All of us have some stubborn streaks – a few issues we refuse to waver on. But for some people stubbornness is a way of life. Such people can be very unapproachable and almost impossible to confront because they approach the world with an "I know it all" attitude. It is difficult to be in relationship with a very stubborn person because listening is not

It is difficult to be in a relationship with a very stubborn person because listening is not something they are very willing to try.

something they are very willing to try. Their defenses are always up since they do not want to see or accept the truth about themselves. A small bump in the road can become a major disagreement because they are unwilling to consider a different perspective. Communication is stifled either because every conversation has to end either with them being right, or "refusing to discuss this any further" when they know they can't win.

Stubbornness presents a major problem in marriages. The stubborn person refuses to take any responsibility when things go wrong, which means the spouse becomes the scapegoat taking the blame for any problems. Two stubborn people in one marriage...that topic may require another book entirely!!

If you tend to become defensive and start making excuses every time a finger is pointed in your direction, you have a problem with stubbornness. Here's a newsflash: everybody sees it but you! If you detect a pattern of failing to keep jobs or maintaining healthy relationships, it may point you to the fact that you are the common denominator at the root of your problems.

Stubbornness is a bigger problem than any of us can get our heads around, but the solution doesn't need to be complicated. Admitting to having this problem is the first step in a truly radical life change. The second step is extremely powerful: Just shut up and start to listen! You don't need to say a word in defense of wrong behavior; seriously! Let someone tell you what's on

If you tend to become defensive and start making excuses every time a finger is pointed in your direction, you have a problem with stubbornness.

their mind without trying to turn it around and making it all about you...again. This is guaranteed to change your life. Finally, act on what you hear! Listening is the key to understanding as we read in Matthew: *"Let him who has ears [to hear] be listening, and let him consider and perceive and understand by hearing"* (Matt. 13:43AMP).

Let's give our life and relationships a chance by really listening the next time someone is trying to give us honest feedback. Friends or foes, God may use both to tell us the very truth we need to hear most. Only by listening, without jumping to our own defense, will we be able to finally see what we haven't been able to see about ourselves before.

> *"To one who listens, valid criticism is like a gold earring or other gold jewelry."*
>
> *Proverbs 25:12 NLT*

Once we really hear what we need to hear, we can change what we need to change.

Chapter 14

CHOICES

This day I call heaven and earth as witnesses against you that I have set before you life and death, blessings and curses. Now choose life, so that you and your children may live.

DEUTERONOMY 30:19 NIV

Every choice we make brings us along life's path in a definitive direction. Our choices either lead us along the path of life and God's blessing, or the path of sin and death. God's will for His children is that we will choose the path of His blessings. God was not the one who set up the option of choosing the curse; Satan was responsible for that. Blessing is God's choice for our lives, at all times, in and through every situation.

Only knowledge of God and His Word can properly equip us to make choices that bring success and blessing. If we know and understand His Word and continue to make wrong choices, we invite destruction into our lives. Our choices are influenced by our beliefs, so if we are to make the right choices in the future, we must be sure to believe what God tells us is true. We can't believe truth we don't know, so choosing to know God's truth should be at the top of the list of making the right choices.

While there may have been exceptional or extreme circumstances resulting from someone else's selfish choices and clearly beyond our control, in this book we deal specifically with the choices that were within our own control.

It stands to reason that if past wrong choices got us into our current messy situations, today's right choices can begin to get us out. Once we commit to knowing God's truth and obeying it, He will give us the strategy we need to find success in every area of life. The following verse shows simply and plainly what our part is in living a successful life:

> This Book of the Law shall not depart out of your mouth, but you shall meditate on it day and night, that you may observe and do according to all that is written in it. For then you shall make your way prosperous, and then you shall deal wisely and have good success (Josh 1:8 AMP).

Our poor choices can be identified quite easily by taking a good look at our current circumstances. If we are overweight and unhealthy, it reveals that we have made poor diet and exercise choices. If we just got fired for the third time, it was likely the result of our choosing bad attitudes and less than excellent work habits.

Recognizing and acknowledging the cause and effect relationships between choices and consequences is a huge step of maturity.

If we can't stand our spouse......guess who chose them. If we are on our third marriage...well, you get the picture.

Recognizing and acknowledging the cause and effect relationships between choices and resulting consequences is a huge step of maturity, and a strong defense against experiencing similar problems in the future.

If we want to see real change in our lives, it does require several steps.

1. Get our mind off what we can't change - completely off!
2. Decide what we have the power to change and focus only on that.
3. Seek God's wisdom for specific steps.
4. Refuse to remain a helpless victim.

Our wrong choices will eventually bring us to a place of crisis when again we will be given a choice to start doing things God's way. The alternative is to become bitter and blame God or others, blinding ourselves once again to an opportunity to experience freedom by facing the truth.

God has set life and death before us; we have to purposely choose life. No matter what we try to tell ourselves we will not escape the results of our choices.

Our beliefs are hidden forces that shape our values and determine our choices.

Our choices position us to experience success or failure. Choosing to seek God's kingdom and His truth brings the wisdom we need to believe right, choose wisely, and have success. The choice to serve God is the most important choice you can make!

> *"But if you refuse to serve the Lord, then choose today whom you will serve."*
>
> *Joshua 24:15 NLT*

What is your life *today* telling you about your past choices? Every time we need to make a choice we should be honest with ourselves about how much it may end up costing.

Chapter 15

CLARE'S STORY

When I met Clare she had been married for thirty years and had been a Christian for twenty-five. Clare went to church and Bible study faithfully. She was as sincere in her faith as anyone I've met, yet she described herself as a bitter woman.

Clare felt she obeyed God faithfully but her marriage didn't show it. She and her husband had no relationship to speak of. She said that communication consisted of them "grunting at each other". She stated that there were many things about him that annoyed her and nothing that she liked. In fact she admitted that she actually hated him. Clare said the only reason she stayed was because she didn't want to disobey God.

According to her, the only thing they did together was the grocery shopping. When I pointed out that many women would give their left arm to have their husband grocery shop with them, she was surprised. I suggested she begin looking at what her husband *did* do rather than what he didn't, and be thankful for that. I pointed out that even though she was serious about her faith, she was not obeying God in the area of respecting her husband, forgiving him for his shortcomings, or having a thankful attitude. Clare granted that this was true, but hadn't considered these to be the BIG problems before. She left our first session agreeing to work on these areas.

When I saw Clare again two weeks later she was so emotional she had difficulty expressing the amazing changes that had been happening in her marriage. She kept shaking her head in disbelief that these dramatic changes were simply the result of her being convicted of truth and then beginning to show her husband some kindness and gratitude. She shared about their wonderful turnaround with tears of joy in her eyes and a look of astonishment on her face.

Clare realized that she had been guilty of pride and of placing unrealistic expectations on her husband instead of appreciating him where he was and trusting God to get him where he needed to be. Clare had been so wrapped up in living her religion that she missed what really mattered to God. She had become increasingly self-righteous and critical over the years instead of more loving and accepting.

> **When I saw Clare again two weeks later she was so emotional she had difficulty expressing the amazing changes that had been happening in her marriage.**

For all those years Clare had believed she was right; that he was the one with all the problems. When God opened her eyes to the simple truth that she had been gathering knowledge but not living what she learned in her home, she repented and their marriage changed quickly and dramatically. Towards the end of this second meeting with Clare, she shuffled to the edge of her seat and asked sincerely if this sudden change happening solely as a result of her finding truth meant that all the fault for things having gone wrong was hers. I assured her that she was only responsible for her own wrong choices; her husband was not absolved of his responsibility just because she became accountable for hers! I explained that her repentance had opened the door for ongoing restoration through the love and grace she was able to extend to him as a result.

Clare said her husband didn't fully understand what had suddenly happened to change things between them so radically, but he was too busy enjoying their new relationship and booking a romantic weekend retreat to care!

The reality is that all the years that Clare had spent getting to know God and His Word had not been wasted, but her deep-rooted bitterness had kept her from receiving the blessings God had for her all along. Her prior motivation in the marriage had been self-seeking (wanting things her way). God's way is to lovingly seek the other's good. The truth she'd learned became real heart knowledge, not just head knowledge when she took personal responsibility and decided to love unconditionally. Clare started living the life she'd wanted once she "just got over herself," changed some wrong beliefs, and found God's perspective.

Part 3

Exposing the Mouth

Words satisfy the mind as much as fruit does the stomach; good talk is as gratifying as a good harvest. Words kill, words give life; they're either poison or fruit—you choose.
Proverbs 18:20-21 MSG

Chapter 16

IMPACT

*A word out of your mouth may seem of no account, but it
can accomplish nearly anything—or destroy it!*

JAMES 3:5 MSG

Words spoken about us, to us and by us impact our lives
so much more than we may realize. Much of the internal
baggage we carry around is a result of negative things that
were spoken to. If we accepted these harmful comments
as truth, meditated on them and made them part of our
belief system, they are still impacting us today. In Part One
we learned how thoughts enter our minds either through
words we hear, or things we see and experience. In Part
Two we learned how beliefs become rooted in our heart
after we meditate on these thoughts and accept them as
truth. In this section we will discover that it is these heart
beliefs and the attitudes that accompany them that flow out
of our mouths through our words.

The reality is that we cannot hide anything in our hearts because sooner or later its contents become evident by the words we speak. We can tell what is in someone's heart by the things they say, and when we speak we give away what's in ours. Jesus teaches about this principle in Luke chapter six:

> *The good man brings good things out of the good stored up in his heart, and the evil man brings evil things out of the evil stored up in his heart. For out of the overflow of his heart his mouth speaks (Luke 6:45 NIV).*

We've probably all been in situations where we have been made to feel small by someone's words. Perhaps we've also made others feel hurt, unaccepted or unappreciated by the words we've spoken. On the other hand, we have also been blessed, encouraged and motivated by words. Hopefully we have edified others in the same way.

The ability to communicate through words sets humans apart from the rest of God's creation. We can speak from the moment we wake up until the moment we fall asleep, although this does seem to be easier for women!

It is significant that in the beginning God brought all the creatures to Adam so he could name them (Gen 2 -19-20 NIV). God by His own word gave authority and dominion over all the earth to man. Right from the beginning man's authority was expressed through words. Adam's first task was to speak a name or identity over the animals.

Other scriptures show us our words also have the potential to bless or to curse. If we can truly grasp the reality of these following verses, they will change the way we talk:

> *"Death and life are in the power of the tongue, those who love it will eat its fruit" (Prov18:21 NKJV).*

James continues Jesus' teaching about the power of the tongue by comparing it to a fire. The smallest spark set off by a carelessly placed word can set off a forest fire. Our speech can *"ruin the world, turn harmony to chaos, throw mud on a reputation, and send the whole world up in smoke"* (James 3:6 MSG).

Jesus' teaching on the power of our words is equally sobering:

> *It's your heart, not the dictionary that gives meaning to your words. A good person produces good deeds and words season after season. An evil person is blight on the orchard. Let me tell you something: Everyone of these careless words is going to come back and haunt you. There will be a time of reckoning. Words are powerful; take them seriously. Words can be your salvation. Words can also be your damnation* (Matt. 12:35-37 MSG).

With His words Jesus also performed miracles. Sometimes He asked questions of those who came to Him for healing. This wasn't because He didn't know the answers, but because He knew the faith released in their answers would open them up to His healing power.

Words are powerful. Every time you speak you make a choice, because your words are determining your experience of life and the health of your relationships. The chapters that follow in this section deal with ways our words can be used either constructively or destructively.

"Watch your words and hold your tongue; you'll save yourself a lot of grief."

Proverbs 21:23 MSG

Avoiding numerous problems may be as simple as knowing when to hold your tongue.

Chapter 17

OPINIONS

*Cultivate your own relationship with God, but don't
impose it on others. You're fortunate if your behavior
and your belief are coherent. But if you're not sure, if
you notice that you are acting in ways inconsistent with
what you believe–some days trying to impose your opinions
on others, other days just trying to please them–then you
know that you're out of line. If the way you live isn't
consistent with what you believe, then it's wrong.*

ROMANS 14:22 MSG

I really wish I had come across this verse within the first
few days of becoming a Christian! It took me many years to
realize that my opinions and the strong stand I thought I
was taking for God were really having the opposite effect
on people. I was zealous and passionate about my new-
found faith in Jesus, but too many of my actions and
motives were still rooted in the old me. I needed to
cultivate my own relationship with God until I had His

heart for others, rather than trying to guilt them into getting right with God through my own opinions. Sometimes being opinionated just means we adopt the wrong methods in an attempt to achieve the right goal. This will not work because people either become offended, feel controlled or, quite frankly want to get away from us.

If we want to invite strife into our life it really is easy - just have lots of unnecessary opinions! Even when we are called on for an opinion, the one who is asking is more likely just looking for agreement with their own opinion rather than any of our views. At other times people ask our opinion because they want to draw us into an argument and prove how clever they are.

> **Sometimes being opinionated just means we adopt the wrong methods in an attempt to achieve the right goal.**

The Pharisees did this a few times with Jesus, but He had them figured out. He knew they were just trying to get Him to say something that they could twist and use against Him. Jesus knew what we still may need to learn about opinions: they can be a prideful misuse of the power of words and won't end with any good result.

Think back to how angry other people's opinions on pointless issues have made you in the past. The truth is that most of the things that we give opinions on do nothing but cause strife between people. Whether it's politics, religion or how to raise children, opinions seldom improve or build relationships. We all know of too many relationships that have been damaged or destroyed because of people freely offering opinions. It bears repeating that sometimes it's wise to just shut up or walk away from people and their opinions before we get drawn in and start adding our own. The book of Proverbs is brimming with warnings concerning fools and their opinions. In chapter 18 it says: *"A [self-confident] fool has no delight in understanding but only in revealing his personal opinions and himself"* (Prov. 18:1-3 AMP).

Do our opinions reveal a foolish disregard for understanding, as the writer of Proverbs says? Once we become honest with ourselves about our purposes in airing our opinions, it will become easier to control the urge and keep them to ourselves.

When we are spiritually weak we tend to be susceptible to the opinions of others. This can leave us in a constant state of confusion, anxiety and insecurity. The only solution is to be firmly grounded in God's Word and to find our identity in Him. This ensures that we will be secure enough to resist being negatively influenced by another's misguided opinions.

The only solution is to be firmly grounded in God's Word and to find our identity in Him.

From time to time it does become necessary to give input. In these situations we should think in terms of giving a different perspective rather than an opinion. This helps people to see things another way and keeps them open to what we are saying without making them feel we are imposing our views on them. When we must give an opinion, let's make sure it is based on God's truth and shared for His purposes out of love and concern for others, never in arrogance or pride.

Opinions may seem to be an insignificant topic to some, but I've seen the results of making a change in this area and they can be astounding. When opinionated people give up this "habit", it very noticeably impacts people who know them because the change is so dramatic and observable. Even in a relatively short time it drastically alters the way people respond to them. Test the wisdom of Proverbs where we read,

*He who has knowledge spares his words, and a man
of understanding has a cool spirit. Even a fool when he
holds his peace is considered wise; when he closes his
lips he is esteemed a man of understanding.*

Proverbs 17:27-29 AMP

If you're an opinionated person looking for change, challenge yourself to stop giving unnecessary opinions at least until you finish this book. You may be pleasantly surprised at what you discover!

Chapter 18

SELF-RIGHTEOUSNESS

We are all infected and impure with sin. When we display our righteous deeds, they are nothing but filthy rags.

ISAIAH 64:6 NLT

Self-righteous people have a way of making others feel that they are not quite hitting the mark. They often make statements like "well I would *never*." You'll hear them using "I" and "me" quite a bit. Self-righteousness was a defining trait of the Pharisees; even Jesus could do no right in their eyes. As Christians, we should be concerned about our own tendency towards self righteousness; it seems an easy trap to fall into. We need to ask ourselves if the standards we impose on others, or our judgments of them, will bring them closer to God or push them further away. Even those who have a desire for relationship with God may be tempted to give up if it appears that they can never measure up to our standards. Jesus reserved His harshest criticism for self-righteous people. He minced no words when He said,

> Woe to you, teachers of the law and Pharisees, you hypocrites! You shut the kingdom of heaven in men's faces. You yourselves do not enter, nor will you let those enter who are trying to (Matt 23:12-14 NIV).

There was a reason Jesus took self-righteousness so seriously. Self-righteous people make others feel filthy, unworthy and hopeless as if they will never be good enough to achieve their impossible standards. Imagine cleaning windows with a dirty rag - that's a picture of what happens when we self-righteously try to tell others how to live! They end up having a harder time seeing the truth!

Self-righteousness is rooted in pride, and when we speak with an attitude of self-righteousness it will never bring the right result because it brings others down.

Self-righteousness is rooted in pride, and when we speak with an attitude of self-righteousness, it will never bring the right result because it brings others down rather than encouraging and motivating them to do right. The writer of Proverbs also warns us about this character flaw: *"A [self-confident] fool's mouth is his ruin, and his lips are a snare to himself"* (Prov 18:7 AMP).

Self-righteous people are deceived into thinking that they stand for God's righteousness. All they are really doing is establishing their own rules for righteousness and demanding that others live up to them. Righteous living cannot be produced in others by directing our anger towards their sinful choices. James tells us that our anger cannot promote the righteousness of God (James 1:20). True righteousness is when we are angered by the pain and loss people suffer as a result of deception and sin. It compels us to encourage, bless, and help them become free.

God is not looking just for outward observable righteous acts, but for a heart that is humble and obedient to Him, filled with love and concern for the well-being of others. This is the kind of right living that allows us to experience more of His power in our own lives and increases the impact we have on others for good.

> *"For I tell you that unless your righteousness surpasses that of the Pharisees and the teachers of the law, you will certainly not enter the kingdom of heaven".*
>
> *Matthew 5:20 NIV*

Our responsibility is to live righteously, NOT to force others to live as we think they should.

Chapter 19

AGREEMENT

Can two people walk together without agreeing on the direction?

AMOS 3:3 NLT

Imagine heading off on vacation with three of your best friends. You arrive at your destination, thinking that everyone would head straight for the beach. Another friend thought everyone would want to go sight-seeing, while yet another planned to go eat. The fourth thought everyone would want to unpack right away and relax. How do you think this vacation is going to turn out unless people begin to agree on what to do collectively? Overlooking the power of agreement is common, yet churches, families and businesses fall apart daily because people lack agreement. Jesus did not overstate things when He warned that *"a house divided against itself cannot stand"* (Mark 3:25 NKJV).

Wars, divorce and rebellion are all results of disagreement, and sin is the result of disagreeing with

God's way of doing things. Yet the power of agreeing with the right things is astounding! Jesus talks of this in Matthew 18 where He says:

> *Again I say to you if any two of you agree on earth concerning anything that they ask, it will be done for them by My Father in heaven. For where two or three are gathered together in my name, I am there in the midst of them (Matt 18: 19-20 NKJV).*

We need to realize that we can't agree with God until we know what His Word says. Our failures in life are evidence of agreeing with the wrong things. Satan is a deceiver and will drop suggestions into our minds continually if we allow it. The great news is that Christ set us free from having to agree with Satan. Amazingly no matter what Satan tries to make us believe, his suggestions have no power over us unless we choose to agree with them! Eve had to agree with Satan that God was withholding good from her or she wouldn't have eaten the fruit. When Jesus was tempted on the Temple Mount by Satan during His forty days of fasting, He disagreed with everything Satan offered by speaking God's Word in response.

Strongholds in our belief systems are broken when we agree with and say what God says. His words are truth and anything that contradicts them is a lie. Specific strongholds need specific truth from Scripture to destroy them. We are responsible to know what the Word says by finding these truths and meditating on them, settling them in our hearts until they pour out of our mouths without thinking. God's kingdom advances through our lives when we know and agree with His plans and ways.

The keys of the kingdom are the knowledge and understanding of God's Word, His ways and His will. Jesus says to His disciples,

I will give you the keys of the kingdom of heaven; and whatever you bind (declare to be improper and unlawful) on earth must be what is already bound in heaven; and whatever you loose (declare lawful) on earth must be what is already loosed in heaven (Matt 16:19 AMP).

When Jesus was tempted by Satan (read Luke 4:1-15) all He used was God's Word. No arguments were necessary. Just stating God's truth gave Him the victory.

God needs people to agree with Him for His will to be established on earth. When we say "Thy will be done," we are saying that no matter how we feel or what we want, we agree that God's will is always the best choice. You may also want to consider carefully who you choose to pray with, and what you choose to pray for.

> **When we say, "Thy will be done," we are saying that no matter how we feel or what we want, we agree that God's will is always the best choice.**

Are you in agreement with God and each other? Surround yourself with people who can agree with you for seeing God's plans realized in your life.

But I urge and entreat you, brethren, by the name of our Lord Jesus Christ, that all of you be in perfect harmony and full agreement in what you say, and that there be no dissensions or factions or divisions among you, but that you be perfectly united in your common understanding and in your opinions and judgments.

1 Corinthians 1:10 AMP

When we agree with anyone about anything, we empower their belief, even when it is a wrong one.

Chapter 20

GRUMBLING AND COMPLAINING

*How long will this evil congregation murmur against
Me? I have heard the complaints the Israelites
murmur against Me.*

NUMBERS 14:27 AMP

Whether we care to admit it or not, anytime a Christian complains they are in effect saying that God cannot be trusted to deliver on His promises. All our complaining is rooted in unbelief and selfishness. The Israelites were a prime example of this as they plodded around in the wilderness for forty years. Despite witnessing one miracle after another we are told that,

> *...they hastily forgot His works; they did not
> [earnestly] wait for His plans [to develop] regarding
> them, but lusted exceedingly in the wilderness and
> tempted and tried to restrain God [with their insistent
> desires] in the desert. And He gave them their*

> request, but sent leanness into their souls and [thinned
> their numbers by] disease and death (Psalm 106:13-
> 15 AMP).

As a counselor I cannot tell you the number of times I've had clients complain about not having enough money for basics such as bread and milk, or not being able to pay their hydro bill. Then they betray themselves moments later by mentioning something they've watched on cable or something that happened at the gym, or saying that they cannot live without their Starbucks every day. They are getting what they want, but suffering as a result. These comments reveal that their grumbling and complaining are a way to get sympathy or something else they want at someone else's expense.

Grumbling and complaining won't stop until we learn to trust God for what we need, and be thankful for what we've been given. We must put

Grumbling and complaining won't stop until we learn to trust God for what we need and be thankful for what we've been given.

what we think we have to have at the bottom of our priority list. We need God's perspective on everything. God hates ungratefulness because it prevents us from seeing both His goodness and our own potential. We cannot experience success as long as we remain selfish, because selfishness limits our vision and blinds us to the possibilities and opportunities God has placed in front of us.

The fourteenth chapter of the Old Testament book of Numbers tells the story of the twelve spies sent by Moses to spy out the land God had promised His people. Ten of these men came back saying that the land was indeed good, but there was no way they could conquer it because its inhabitants made them feel like grasshoppers. Clearly they were having difficulty remembering the size of their God and what He had already done for them! Look at how their grumbling and complaining infected the whole congregation:

> *And the men whom Moses sent to search the land…*
> *returned and made all the congregation grumble and*
> *complain against him by bringing back a slanderous*
> *report of the land. Even those men who brought the evil*
> *report of the land died by a plague before the Lord. But*
> *Joshua son of Nun and Caleb son of Jephunneh, who*
> *were among the men who went to search the land, lived*
> *still (Num. 14:36-38 AMP).*

Joshua and Caleb saw the same things the others saw, but their faith in God gave them a completely different perspective and attitude. Incidentally, they were the only two of the original adult generation freed from Egypt that actually made it to the Promised Land. If we knew grumbling and complaining had a negative payoff, we'd never do it!

> *"Do all things without grumbling and faultfinding*
> *and complaining [against God] and questioning and*
> *doubting [among yourselves]."*
>
> Philippians 2:14 AMP

Be really honest with yourself about how you think your grumbling and complaining benefits you. Choose to adopt an attitude of gratitude today!

Chapter 21

DEFENSIVENESS

*If we claim to be without sin we deceive ourselves and
the truth is not in us.*

1 JOHN 1:8 NIV

There is a possibility that the issue of defensiveness has become less of a problem in your life since you began reading this book. Several times I have recommended that you choose to shut up and listen if you really want to learn the truth and change. If you are still defending yourself by making excuses, justifying your behaviour, or blaming others you obviously haven't taken that advice to heart yet, so here's another opportunity to do so!

If your habit in the past has been to jump to your own defense by trying to explain why you said or did something that is being addressed, it will take practice to say nothing and begin to give serious consideration to what has been said.

Take a few moments to think about who you really are. Are you allowing your clothes, friends, job, financial status or accomplishments to define you? All these sources are unstable and will breed insecurity in you if you depend on them for your sense of worth. You can't always have the latest fashion, the best job, all the stuff you want, or even your friendships, as they too will come and go. If you find your identity in such unstable sources you will slip into defensive mode any time someone challenges your choices.

> **Are you allowing your clothes, friends, job, financial status or accomplishments to define you?**

Behind defensiveness lies insecurity. This is why we try desperately to make others see things our way. If they don't, it shatters our confidence in who we are and what we believe. Since our identity comes from who or what we identify with, we will attempt to defend the source because our self-worth is so wrapped up in it. The great thing about finding your identity in Christ is that it takes the pretense out of living. You're not perfect but you are unconditionally loved and accepted; your worth is no longer based on what you possess or accomplish.

Satan always challenges our confidence and security by attacking our belief in God. His questions make us doubt and question God's desire to be good to us. So the only thing you need to defend is your belief, and you do it the same way Jesus did: "It is written" or "God says…" God's Word has the power to settle any issue.

We choose whether to be thankful, to complain, or to be defensive. We choose whether to remain in the desert and die there, or to walk free. Change happens when we do the right things we haven't been doing, or stop doing the wrong things we have been doing. Change happens to those who are teachable and humble enough to take advice, not those who are closed-minded.

Paul warns the Christians at Ephesus about the dangers of being closed-minded. The minds of unteachable people are "full of darkness" and "far from the life God gives" (Eph 4:17:19). Closed-minded people are not only unteachable, they are also deceived. God wants us to be free of all deception. Pray and ask Him to reveal the root cause of your defensive behaviours. Sometimes defensive behaviour results from hurts and fears inflicted through childhood experiences. Shedding the light of God's truth on those areas will bring healing and understanding where we most need it. The Psalmist says, *"The entrance of Your words gives light; It gives understanding to the simple"* (Psalm 119:129 NKJV). When we are open-minded, understanding comes.

If you continually feel the need to defend your behaviour and your choices, how righteous can they really be?

If you continually feel the need to defend your behaviour and your choices, how righteous can they really be? When we are living right, we don't need to apologize, explain, or defend ourselves to anyone. Being defensive becomes unnecessary! If we are wrongly accused we know that God will defend us.

And will not [our just] God defend and protect and avenge His elect (His chosen ones), who cry to Him day and night? Will He defer them and delay help on their behalf?

Luke 18:7 AMP.

Self-defense may be good exercise for the body, but not for the mind.

Chapter 22

NICOLE'S STORY

When I first met Nicole she admitted she was plagued with anxieties. She had long "to do" lists - both written and mental - that she never conquered. Nicole told me she had been insecure since she was a little child. Nicole was the youngest of three children and often felt alone, fearing that her parents wouldn't return from work and that she would be left alone.

As an adult Nicole couldn't feel secure unless everything was done the way she wanted. Needless to say this was an unrealistic expectation and put a great deal of pressure on her relationships. Things seldom (if ever) got done to her satisfaction, so she remained constantly insecure and fearful. Nicole wrongly believed that controlling her environment by telling others what to do and how to do it, would give her the security she sought. Her instruction and correction was constant and mostly negative. Nicole felt compelled to give her opinion in almost every situation, which led to constant tension and arguments in her marriage.

Nicole's life began to change for the better the day she began to exchange her wrong beliefs with faith actions.

This required choosing to trust God in every situation and not giving in to her feelings of fear that things would go wrong if she didn't say something. In Nicole's case this meant keeping her opinions to herself and allowing the people close to her the freedom to do things their own way, without any "help" from her.

Nicole realized that if she wanted to have peace in her life and relationships she had to concede that most of her opinions were really just her perspective, not the final word as she had previously assumed. She realized her opinions constantly caused disagreements and did not create the peaceful environment she so wanted. These endless opinions about many unimportant matters also made her appear self-righteous – not the impression she wanted people to have of her since she was a genuinely loving and caring person. People began to respond to Nicole very differently when she began to behave according to her changed beliefs.

While she admits that it's not always easy, she sees the positive effects of changing these attitudes in her life daily. She has learned that her attempts to control with her opinions often got in the way of what God wanted to do in her life. When people were frustrated with her, they weren't so anxious to know about her God. When Nicole managed to "just get over herself" by giving up her right to constantly voice her opinion, and trust that others could make good decisions without her constant input, she stopped frustrating those around her. She was finally able to relax, and they were at last able to see and appreciate her for the wise and considerate woman she truly is.

> **She has learned that her attempts to control with her opinions often got in the way of what God wanted to do in her life.**

Part Four

<u>Exposing Your Potential</u>

*Oh yes, you shaped me first inside, then out;
you formed me in my mother's womb. I thank you,
High God—you're breathtaking!
Body and soul, I am marvelously made! I
worship in adoration—what a creation! You know
me inside and out, you know every bone in my body;
You know exactly how I was made, bit by bit, how
I was sculpted from nothing into something.
Like an open book, you watched me grow from
conception to birth; all the stages of my life were
spread out before you, the days of my life all
prepared before I'd even lived one day.
(Psalm 139: 13-15 MSG)*

Chapter 23

PERSONALITY

*For we are God's masterpiece. He has created us
anew in Christ Jesus so we can do the good things
He planned for us long ago.*

EPHESIANS 2:10 NLT

For those of us who have struggled with self-image (really, who hasn't?) we may need help to understand who we really are. You are the only you there ever was or will ever be. When we have children we easily understand that we don't want them all to be the same; we love and celebrate their differences and distinctiveness. God is just the same with us. He wants us to recognize and appreciate His masterful work in creating us in a unique way for a unique purpose. If we don't recognize who we really are, we can't know what we've really been created to do. If you had never seen a DVD player before you might mistake it for a sophisticated toaster. This wouldn't do the bread or the DVD player much good now would it? This kind of misidentification has happened to everyone at some time and to some degree. Until we are able to recognize our own worth and value it can be difficult for others to see it, because we project who we think we are. We may struggle with being misunderstood, mistreated, misused, and even abused when we or others attempt to fit us into moulds we were never intended to fit into. The more aware we become of God's purpose for our lives the less likely we are to misuse ourselves or allow others to misuse us.

I grew up in a family of gentle, kind and low-key people. Since I wasn't like that, no one really knew quite what to expect from me. Too be honest, I never really knew what to expect from myself either! I liked to talk, just for the sake of it. Keeping my thoughts and opinions to myself

> **Until we are able to recognize our own worth and value it can be difficult for others to see it, because we project who we think we are.**

was an option I seemed largely unaware of! Unfortunately, like most people who don't understand that they alone are responsible for their actions, I decided that this was just who I was and nothing was ever going to change it. As for other people… well they would just have to like it or lump it!

Beginning to understand my own personality brought me much-needed understanding and insight. I began recognizing that we all have strengths, but there are right and wrong ways to use them. Learning to understand personality differences confirmed what I already knew: I had a big mouth without a built-in tactfulness monitor. I liked to tell stories and amuse people. I also loved to encourage, inspire and motivate people – that is, the ones I actually liked. For the people I wasn't so fond of, that very same mouth could just as effectively criticize, judge and condemn.

After God began to reveal these issues that needed change, I discovered the truth, that I had more control over my mouth than I had previously thought, I could actually decide what to say or not to say. God had gifted me to communicate, but until my mouth came under His control rather than my own, I would continue to wreak havoc with it.

Allowing our own will to determine how to use our God-given strengths can sadly turn them into our greatest weaknesses, working against God's purposes rather than for them. I was finally able to see and admit that I didn't have to voice every mindless thought. I realized that while I was determined to use my mouth my way by saying whatever I wanted with little or no regard for the feelings of others, I was hurting people more than I was helping them. While this was probably the biggest discovery for me, there were other weaknesses I became conscious of, such as my lack of discipline and impatience. When you become self-aware you acknowledge both the good and the bad. You become empowered to change what you need to change.

Have you ever noticed that the most appealing people are usually the ones who are aware of their weaknesses and limitations and don't feel the need to hide them?

Have you ever noticed that the most appealing people are usually the ones who are aware of their weaknesses and limitations and don't feel the need to hide them? Instead, they have learned to accept themselves as they are while continuing to submit to God's transforming process. We all have weaknesses and we all need transforming. Being aware of the strengths and weaknesses of different personality types helps us understand, relate, and communicate better with people who are different than us.

What follows is a lighthearted look at the four basic personality types. It can be insightful and helpful in relationships, but is not to be taken too seriously. No one type is better or worse than any other, and each type has distinctive strengths and weaknesses. Everyone will be a blend of at least two to varying degrees. Have fun with it, but don't be tempted to label and box everyone you know. Keep in mind: no two people are the same!

In the beginning God created...

The Party Seekers,
The Power Seekers,
The Perfection Seekers and
The Peace Seekers.

The **Party Seekers** are the life of the party, optimistic and outgoing. Variety is the spice of life for them. They also like to live in the moment rather than plan for tomorrow. They love to talk, tell stories, and are typically very social. These are just a few of their wonderful qualities, but until God gets a hold of them they will try to dominate conversations and may tend to be undisciplined, unreliable, naïve, and loud. They

> **Party Seekers are the most important person in their own world.**

often speak without thinking, won't think twice about interrupting others and will be the most important person in their own world. This is why it's easy for them to forget things like your name, your birthday, where they were supposed to meet you for lunch, and other small details like where they may have parked the car.

Remember big-mouthed Peter? Full of zeal, bravado and passion one minute then lying and hiding the next! His life was a great example of what can happen when "Party Seekers" surrender their will to God (Heb 12:6 & 1 Cor 3:15).

In order to reach their best potential the Party Seekers need to develop some humility, peace and patience and a good dose of self control.

The world would be so dull without the Party Seeker!

Next we have the **Power Seekers**. I know the name kind of gives it away but people with this personality are productive, highly organized, bold, confident, determined, independent, goal-oriented and natural leaders. It's easy for this group to achieve success as they are highly motivated and driven to succeed. Very task-oriented, they tend to be impatient with mere mortals of other personalities. At their worst they can be bossy, controlling, confrontational, unsympathetic "know it all" types who don't take correction well because they struggle with pride and a sense of superiority. In fact, they don't really need other people much anyway but will tolerate the kind that will do their bidding. Understand that they aren't intentionally out to hurt people; being so goal- focused just causes them to be somewhat insensitive to the feelings of others. These are the world's movers and shakers.

> **Very task-oriented, they tend to be impatient with mere mortals of other personalities.**

When the Power Seeker types develop some gentleness, meekness, kindness and a lot of patience they can work effectively with others and find the success they desire without sacrificing relationships in the process.

Remember how awful Saul was (Acts 8-9) until God did the blindness number on him and changed him into the Apostle Paul? Paul ended up writing most of the New Testament! He fearlessly spread the gospel, stopping at nothing, not even stoning, snakebites or shipwrecks!

How much would we actually get done without the Power Seeker?

Next we have the **Perfection Seekers**. These talented and sensitive people provide the world with much of its artistic beauty. They are creative, detailed and sensitive; they are list-makers who have a love of information. They are also disciplined, orderly and controlled. In relationships they can tend toward suspicion and caution and do not trust easily or quickly. They can also tend to be moody, negative and hold on to hurts. They may withhold affection to punish those who hurt them. Some of the challenges for

> **They are disciplined, orderly and controlled.**

the Perfection Seeker group include being overly analytical, hard to please and nit-picky, which can make life frustrating for them because not everyone aspires to their high standards. Their tender hearts are also high on compassion and they easily sacrifice themselves for those in need.

Perfection Seekers generally need to develop more joy, peace, love, and humility. Choosing to focus on the positive and forgiving quickly when they feel hurt or offended will make a huge difference in their day-to-day life experience.

King David showed several of these traits. He was gifted musically and wrote many Psalms which beautifully show his love and dependence on God. Though at times he struggled with depression, he would purposely chose to focus on God and His faithfulness through worshiping and praising (Psalm 13).

Perfection Seekers have genius potential! Where would we be without the beauty they bring to the world for the rest of us to enjoy?

Lastly we have the relaxed, easy-to-get-along-with **Peace Seekers**. They are warm, friendly, kind and patient. They like to avoid conflict and confrontation, and can be a lot of fun with their low-key humour. They are the most easy-going of all the personalities – at least until you try to convince them to do something they don't want to do! Then they stubbornly dig in their heels with a smile on

> **They like to avoid conflict and confrontation, and can be a lot of fun with their low-key humour.**

their face, knowing you can scream and shout to try and get your own way, but they are confident that they will never give in. Their lack of enthusiasm and motivation can be discouraging for others, and at times they can take life a little too easy, putting too many things off until tomorrow.

Peace Seekers may need to develop some love, faith, goodness and discipline to fulfill their purpose and enjoy the very best God has in store for them.

I suspect that peace-loving Abraham was a good example of this personality type. The Bible tells of times he went out of his way to avoid conflict. We see an example of that, when he gave his nephew Lot first choice when dividing up the land (Gen 13:8).

The Peace Seeker group is the easiest to get along with. Everybody needs some friends like these!

As you can see, each group has great strengths and its fair share of spiritual weaknesses. When we surrender these to God, He shows us how to develop the spiritual fruits of love, joy, peace, patience, kindness, goodness, faithfulness, gentleness, and self-control (Gal 5:22-23) so each of us can operate to our best ability.

Surrendering our will to God is not just about giving Him our weaknesses. If we depend too much on our personality strengths we can become prideful and independent, which takes us out of the will and purpose of God. The following verse shows what wonderful things we can expect if we choose God's way rather than our own:

> *But what happens when we live God's way? He brings gifts into our lives, much the same way that fruit appears in an orchard—things like affection for others, exuberance about life, serenity. We develop a willingness to stick with things, a sense of compassion in the heart, and a conviction that a basic holiness permeates things and people. We find ourselves involved in loyal commitments, not needing to force our way in life, able to marshal and direct our energies wisely (Gal 5:22 MSG).*

Don't make excuses for your weaknesses. Instead, allow God to exhibit His strength through them. Understanding personalities helps us appreciate and accept ourselves and others. It is surprising just how much more patience and understanding we can develop when we realize that not everybody thinks like we do. God has purposely designed us this way so that we can both complement each other and compensate for one another's weaknesses. We achieve our maximum potential when we work together for the benefit of all. Consider the different personalities of Jesus' first disciples. God used each one in unique and amazing ways even while they were being transformed. He desires to do the same with you.

> *"Put on your new nature, created to be like God—*
> *truly righteous and holy."*
>
> *Ephesians 4:24 NLT*

God loves us just as we are, but He also wants us to become all He created us to be.

Chapter 24

SPIRITUAL GIFTS

*Each person is given something to do that shows who
God is. Everyone gets in on it, everyone benefits. All
kinds of things are handed out by the Spirit, and to all
kinds of people! The variety is wonderful...*

1 CORINTHIANS 12:7-11 MSG

If you are anything like me you may have found it
difficult at times to figure out where you fit in or what you
are actually good at. Some of you may even feel you have
nothing of value to contribute because you lack education
or experience. Fortunately for us God does not choose
favorites. He has given each of us gifts and He desires that
we use them for His purposes. The apostle Paul talks about
gifting at great length. In his letter to the Corinthians Paul
explains that even though there are different gifts, different
ministries and different outcomes, God's Spirit is behind
them all. Spiritual gifts are the special way in which God
equips each believer to serve. Since we are most fulfilled

and effective when operating in our proper role, it's important to discover what our gifts are while

| Since we are most fulfilled and effective when operating in our proper role, it's important to discover what our gifts are. |

understanding that there are no cookie-cutter formulas for serving within our gifting. There are many pastors, but no two teach or lead their churches in exactly the same way. Their personal experience, personality, influences, and gifting all come into play. Scripture likens gifting to body parts in order to show how things are meant to work together.

> *Just as our bodies have many parts and each part has a special function, so it is with Christ's body. We are many parts of one body, and we all belong to each other. In His grace, God has given us different gifts for doing certain things well (Rom. 12:4-6 NLT).*

Just imagine for a moment how wonderful it would be if each of us recognized the importance of the following: we are one little part of a huge body, and each one of us matters so much to the others! There can be no place for pride when everyone has gifts that everyone else needs! If we step on a toe or refuse to offer a helping hand, we all suffer for it. This should inspire us not only to exercise our own gifts through submitting them to God's purpose, but also to encourage everyone else to do likewise. Just as we are all important to God, so also we should be to each other.

> *I want you to think about how all this makes you more significant, not less. A body isn't just a single part blown up into something huge. It's all the different-but-similar parts arranged and functioning together. If Foot said, "I'm not elegant like Hand, embellished with rings; I guess I don't belong to this body," would that make it so? If Ear said, "I'm not*

*beautiful like Eye, limpid and expressive; I don't
deserve a place on the head," would you want to
remove it from the body? If the body was all eye, how
could it hear? If all ear, how could it smell? As it is,
we see that God has carefully placed each part of the
body right where he wanted it.*

1 Corinthians 12:14-18 MSG

Discover your God-given spiritual gifts and begin serving in the unique and wonderful way you were designed to.

Chapter 25

RELEASING YOUR PASSION

*And now, isn't it wonderful all the ways in which this
distress has goaded you closer to God? You're more
alive, more concerned, more sensitive, more reverent, more
human, more passionate, more responsible.*

2 CORINTHIANS 7:11 MSG

You cannot be truly passionate about life until you are
passionate about being your true self. The most passionate
and inspiring people are those who take responsibility for
their actions and are honest about who they are with no
pretense. There is nothing as freeing or frightening as
admitting your weaknesses and failures. There is nothing as
oppressive as trying to hide them. Telling yourself the truth
about yourself does set you free to live passionately! Many
of the topics we addressed in earlier chapters relate to
issues we may want to hide from others. As we have seen,
we can pay a heavy price for self deception. It takes so
much time, energy, and effort to hide our weakness and

failures that we may have nothing left to be passionate with.

Many years ago I attended a wedding of some close friends. Back in those days, gossiping was as acceptable to me as breathing. In the case of this couple it just happened that the wife came from a very wealthy family and there were a fair number of rumours going around that the wealth was a big part of the attraction for the groom (completely unfounded of course, because the wife was lovely in every way). Later that day the groom's speech put an end to the gossip and whispers more effectively than I could ever have imagined.

> **Nothing we've ever done comes as a surprise to God, and yet there is a freedom that comes from confessing our sin to Him.**

During his speech he flamboyantly listed off some of the visible assets of the family he had just become a member of, laughingly staking his claim to them.

Now what do you suppose happened to all the whispers then? To tell you the truth, I don't remember it being gossiped about much after that! There is just something amazing and freeing about being honest.

Nothing we've ever done comes as a surprise to God and yet there is a freedom that comes from confessing our sin to Him. While I don't suggest we are required to stand and confess everything to everybody, I do believe transparency is necessary to expose anything that keeps us from living freely and passionately. This leaves us free to live without being weighed down by guilt and shame.

Telling the truth has an amazing effect. It can knock the wind out of the sails of anger, gossip, speculation and our own guilt. Sometimes it's as simple as saying "Yes I did it, I'm guilty." (I did say simple, not easy.) I'm sure we can all think of a few high-profile figures that would have faired better had they chosen truth and admitted their human failings rather than making excuses and trying to cover up shameful secrets. In the end this just makes others more determined to expose the truth.

Living honestly before God is the key to living passionately. The energy we once spent covering up can be transferred to living authentically, freely exercising our gifts, building the body of Christ and advancing the kingdom.

What issues in your life do you still need to come clean about? Start by being honest with yourself, then confessing all to God. In relationships, a sincere apology such as saying "I'm sorry, I did it" can be powerful and put an end to a lot of disagreements.

> *God can do anything, you know—far more than you could ever imagine or guess or request in your wildest dreams! He does it not by pushing us around but by working within us, his Spirit deeply and gently within us.*
>
> *Ephesians 3:20 MSG*

Confessing all to God gets us out of His way. It's easy to live passionately when we realize that He can surpass even our wildest dreams!

Chapter 26

VISION

Write the vision and make it plain on tablets, that he may run who reads it.

HABAKKUK 2:2 NKJV

Somewhere in our hearts and minds exists a hazy vision of the things life has in store for us. It has been marred and blurred by past experiences, labels we've been given, and mostly by what we've believed. We will subconsciously follow the path this vision lays out for our lives. We will make choices, accept beliefs and follow patterns that will continually work to establish this vision, no matter what the vision is or where it came from.

The prostitute on the street, the cocaine addict, the person who steals to survive, they all have a common problem. None of them possess the right vision for their lives. If they could see and believe the possibilities God has for them, they would not be in such a hopeless state. Nevertheless God always has a way out, no matter how desperate the situation may appear. He can give us His vision to lift us out and on to something better.

When we accept God's gift of salvation through Christ, it makes His vision for our lives attainable and available to us. The clearer His vision becomes in our hearts and minds, the more powerfully it can affect and direct our lives, and the less impact our former beliefs will have. The limit we set on what is possible for our lives is determined by our inner (or self) image. When we begin acquiring God's vision for our lives, it starts to change our faulty inner image and we will see more of what is possible as we follow His direction.

> **When we begin acquiring God's vision for our lives, it starts to change our faulty inner image and we will see more of what is possible as we follow His direction.**

The clearer God's vision becomes to us, the easier it is to overcome the temptations that try to keep us from realizing it. If we have a stronger vision of ourselves slim and healthy than we have of the donut or french fries in front of us, it will keep us motivated until we reach the goals we've set. If we have a vision of ourselves married to a wonderful person who loves and cherishes us the way they should, we won't settle for someone who just wants to use us for their own selfish pleasure.

All of us have, at times, had glimpses in our minds of what we could be; most of us sadly never get there. God-given vision is not the same thing as personal ambition. It is not focused on personal success, but on a purpose that improves the circumstances of others while giving us the greatest fulfillment. God gives us the ability to believe for more than we ever thought possible. When we share and believe in His vision and purpose for our lives, we lift the limits off our own idea of what is possible.

A powerful vision directs decisions. That's why it's easier to lose weight for a special occasion; we get a strong image of ourselves walking down the aisle or into the High School reunion looking a certain way. This new self-image overpowers the image we currently have of ourselves, and it becomes possible because we believe it is attainable. But this is only a short term vision. When God's vision of our destiny and calling invades our everyday existence, overcoming becomes a secondary issue. The vision will give us the strength and faith to overwhelm fleshly desires and temptations.

The story of Joseph is one of the greatest biblical examples of what God can do in the life of a person who grasps the vision God gives them and refuses to let go, no matter what the circumstances. Joseph prospered in life because no matter where he was, the pit, the prison, even Pharaoh's palace, He never

The vision God shows us is always superior to anything we could have imagines on our own.

lost sight of who God was or the destiny that God had revealed to him in his dreams (Read Genesis 37: 5-7).

The life we've lived to this point is proof of the vision we've had. If we don't like where we are right now, we need God to give us a glimpse of what He has in store. The vision God shows is always superior to anything we could have imagined on our own. At first it may look ridiculously impossible but the more we grow in faith the more possible it begins to appear.

Vision inspires action. As we act on our vision we become people of purpose. People with a clear vision experience the most success. They don't waste time wondering what they should be doing. If something lines up with the vision, they just get busy doing it. Whatever you focus on determines how you use your time, energy, and resources. This is why allowing God's vision to steer the direction of your life is so important.

Recording the vision and declaring it establishes it firmly in our hearts. When this happens, the decisions we make will line up with the vision. Whether it's choosing the company we keep, what we eat, what we choose to do for a living, which church we decide to attend, who to marry, or what we decide to read and study. We feed and grow our vision by making choices that educate us and prepare us for fulfilling it. If you dream of being a doctor, it's a waste of time going to law school. Vision eliminates unnecessary sidetracking. Our subconscious should continually ask the question "is this choice going to take me in the direction of my God-given vision?" Visions can fail because of distractions, poor choices or how we spend our time. It will take faith in God's good plan for you to line your decisions and resources up with His vision for your life.

> *"Where there is no vision [no redemptive revelation of God], the people perish; but he who keeps the law [of God, which includes that of man]--blessed (happy, fortunate, and enviable) is he."*
>
> *Proverbs 29:18 AMP*

You will never be too old to seek God's vision for your life. As long as you are breathing He has a purpose for you.

Chapter 27

Tracy's Story

Tracy possessed a good balance of two personality types: she was outgoing and enjoyed working with people, but she was also very task-oriented. Tracy's education was in psychology and she had been working for several years as a counselor where the focus was on people and their emotional or relational problems. While she had pursued this line of study believing that it suited her, she eventually began to feel like a square peg in this "round hole" environment. The task-oriented part of her personality remained largely unfulfilled. She just couldn't find the same kind of satisfaction some of the other counselors she worked with did. This confused her as she really wasn't sure what else she was more suited to. Tracy felt frustrated and unsure of what else she could do that would bring her more satisfaction with the education and experience she had.

As we began to explore her strengths and passions, I discovered that she had an incredible talent for budgeting. Her eyes would light up when she talked about it; it got her stirred up like nothing else. The day I realized how unique she was, was when she told me that she wouldn't even buy a pack of gum while at the mall, unless she'd budgeted for it! (If this sounds too radical, you need to keep reading).

I had the advantage of having an insider's view of her life. Although she and her husband didn't earn a lot, they had no credit card debt. They lived well, had a great house with a pool, and two good vehicles. They vacationed at least twice a year and had all three of their kids in extra-curricular activities.

When Tracy walked through the mall she didn't say to herself "it's just a pack of gum, only a couple of bucks" like most of us would. She would look at it and say "I'd rather have my new car and my vacation in Mexico, thanks. Gum, you just aren't worth that much to me." She had an outstanding ability to put financial things into perspective. We determined that this was the gift she needed to share with the world.

As we joined the pieces of her personality, gifts and passions to her personal experiences, her vision really began to take shape. The "people" side of her still wanted to help others, so when she put that skill together with the task of helping people budget, she finally found the satisfaction and success she'd been looking for. Being aware of just how stressed people and relationships are because of mismanaged finances, she started helping people individually with their money management. In following her vision, Tracy also developed and taught seminars on the topic of budgeting. She even started a blog and got published in a magazine. The more she pursued this type of counseling and saw the positive results in people's lives, the more she enjoyed it. She researched which jobs are available for someone with her educational background and a love of budgeting and helping people. She now works as a financial counselor, helping people get out of debt and avoid bankruptcy.

> **As we began to explore her strengths and passions, I discovered that she had an incredible talent for budgeting.**

When it comes to establishing our true identity, it's important to know who we are not, as well as who we are.

Part Five

EXPOSING GOD'S WILL FOR YOU

*In view of all this, make every effort to respond
to God's promises.
Supplement your faith with a generous
provision of moral excellence,
and moral excellence with knowledge,
and knowledge with self-control,
and self-control with patient endurance,
and patient endurance with godliness,
and godliness with brotherly affection,
and brotherly affection with love for everyone.*
1 Peter 1:5-7 NLT

Chapter 28

PREVENTION

If you fully obey the Lord your God and carefully keep all his commands that I am giving you today, the Lord your God will set you high above all the nations of the world. You will experience all these blessings if you obey the Lord your God.

DEUTERONOMY 28:1-2 NLT

In previous chapters we have examined many scriptures and biblical principles that have helped us recognize how often our own choices have ushered in negative consequences. Hopefully this has helped us recognize the power we have been given through our relationship with Jesus to choose how we experience our earthly life. In reality, we always have two choices: doing things God's way, (submitting to His will) or doing it our own way. Either way, we are still the ones who choose.

Future problems are preventable only to the degree that we acknowledge our own responsibility for past problems. Any past wrong behaviours and choices that we attempt to justify will be repeated. Essentially we are holding on to our right to repeat this behavior whenever we feel like it. For example, someone who justifies their anger by blaming it on others is doomed to repeat the behavior. It is difficult to change the outcomes unless we learn to accept our responsibility.

Many people flounder and stumble through life, never knowing that God created them for a specific purpose. They will never be more fulfilled or satisfied than when they follow His will for them. When we are in God's will, we can have confidence in receiving His promises.

God's promises are, of course, conditional. We are responsible for knowing His will and choosing to obey it. This is the only way we can prevent experiencing unnecessary problems.

Not all problems and challenges are preventable, of course. There are certain struggles we will go through because God knows what we need to mature and grow stronger so we can fulfill our destiny. It is the same as when we have to stand back and watch our children struggle to learn a new skill or life lesson. We don't like seeing them suffer, but we know that it is the right and loving thing to do so that they can learn what they need to live life successfully.

Some circumstances are truly beyond our control to change, but if we focus on what cannot be changed we become victims of our circumstances. We need to realize that there is always something in us that God can change no matter what the outside circumstances appear to be, something that helps us rise above what we are facing. The circumstance might not change, but our reaction to it can.

One common definition of insanity is to keep doing what we've always done and expecting a different result. If we want life to change we must be open to seeing what God wants to reveal to us concerning any wrong beliefs or wrong behaviours we are blind to. If we aren't aware of them we can't change them. King David recognized his need for God's help to see what he couldn't see by himself:

> *Search me [thoroughly], O God, and know my heart!*
> *Try me and know my thoughts! And see if there is any*
> *wicked or hurtful way in me, and lead me in the way*
> *everlasting (Psalm 139: 23-24 AMP).*

David's desire to expose his blind spots was so strong that he was willing to become totally vulnerable before God. While it can be difficult to accept and face our own sin, the consequences of not being humble and open enough to do so are much more difficult to deal with. Sin is not something we get away with, although it may initially seem that we do. Sooner or later we will pay the price.

The biggest problem we have is our inability to see the cause and effect relationship in our choices. God's wisdom gives us the ability to see the connection. This is how prevention works: we stop making choices that bring results we don't want to deal with. Getting on track with God saves us from self- inflicted suffering! We stop sowing seeds that we don't want to reap a harvest from later. There is no better prevention than that. The Apostle Paul offers a sobering warning regarding the seeds we sow into our own lives. His admonition leaves no wiggle room:

> *"Do not be deceived and deluded and misled; God will*
> *not allow Himself to be sneered at (scorned, disdained,*
> *or mocked by mere pretensions or professions, or by*
> *His precepts being set aside.) [He inevitably deludes*
> *himself who attempts to delude God.] For whatever a*
> *man sows, that and that only is what he will reap."*

> *Galatians 6:7 AMP*

It is not God's will that you suffer because of ignorance. Become vulnerable and ask Him to search your heart.

Chapter 29

HABITS

Those who live according to the sinful nature have their minds set on what that nature desires; but those who live in accordance with the Spirit have their minds set on what the Spirit desires.

ROMANS 8:5 NIV

Adopting the right habits is a crucial element in fulfilling our purpose and destiny. Many people fall into wrong habit patterns because they fail to use their time and energy in the right ways. For instance, falling into the habit of eating too much fast food happens when we don't feel like taking the time to plan menus, shop, and prepare healthy meals.

We maintain bad habits because they offer familiarity, comfort, and temporary satisfaction. We also fear the unknown results that change would bring, perhaps doubting we will have the ability to deal with the unfamiliar circumstances (all the extra work). Giving in to a habit can bring immediate though temporary relief from stress or anxiety. It's much faster and easier to go to the drive thru.

Unfortunately, continuing to give in to the easy solution also prevents us from getting to the real cause of our stress. Perhaps there are emotional issues we are avoiding, or perhaps we are just being lazy. Maintaining bad habits gives us more reasons to be anxious. (Another negative emotion we will want to avoid). For instance, eating too much fast food can be expensive as well as unhealthy. We become trapped in a vicious cycle of causing anxiety and then feeding anxiety. The worst part is that we lose more and more self-respect every time we give in.

> **Bad habits suck up emotional energy, stifle creativity and imagination, and restrict our ability to believe God for dreams to be realized.**

The longer we maintain harmful habits, the more difficult it becomes to believe that change is possible. Bad habits suck up emotional energy; they stifle creativity and imagination, and restrict our ability to believe God for dreams to be realized. Bad habits get in the way of big dreams.

Poor choices made repeatedly are behind many of our problems and failures. The resulting issues of weight or health, as well as financial issues can affect our relationships negatively. Poor self-image results from failure to break bad habits, making us even more susceptible to believing lies about ourselves. It becomes a vicious cycle.

We can change our habits radically just by changing what we say "yes" to and what we say "no" to. Changing harmful habits means choosing to say "no" to wrong things and "yes" to the right things until the right choice becomes our new habit. This way we get to experience freedom for the rest of our lives. Change begins the moment we acknowledge our need of it and begin to act.

Possessing a clear vision of what life can be like beyond this habit encourages us by drawing us forward, dangling the proverbial carrot, as it were. It draws us forward ever closer to the goal of freedom, giving us the courage to expose the damaging beliefs that are keeping us in bondage. We can set ourselves up for lasting change by immersing ourselves in truth and acting as we would when we've beaten the habit. Facing truth and taking personal responsibility takes away our need to distract ourselves because we are no longer trying to hide anything. Many people only need to change one habit to achieve the success they dream of.

We must ask ourselves if we are ready to leave the familiarity and false sense of security these old habits seem to provide. The real question we need to ask ourselves is not so much "why do I keep sabotaging my life with these bad habits" as "why do I disobey and keep myself out of God's will and away from His blessings?"

Harmful habits are created when we believe that the wrong things can bring lasting happiness or satisfaction. Good habits are created when we trust and believe that a life of obedience and trust in God's great plan will provide more excitement, joy, and satisfaction than we could ever imagine. You can believe and choose your way to your dreams.

> *Strip yourselves of your former nature [put off and discard your old unrenewed self] which characterized your previous manner of life and becomes corrupt through lusts and desires that spring from delusion...*
>
> *Ephesians 4:22 AMP*

Maintaining bad habits multiplies problems. It's God's will that you be free from all your destructive habits because they are taking up His space in your heart.

Chapter 30

HUMILITY

*God opposes the proud but favors the humble. So
humble yourselves before God. Resist the devil, and he
will flee from you. Come close to God, and God will
come close to you.*

JAMES 4:6-8 NLT

Humility is recognizing your true position before God
and admitting that you don't know better than Him.
Humility keeps us open and teachable; it drives us to God
when we need answers. Every day we make dozens of
choices between God's will and our own and between
obedience and sin. Every choice has a consequence. God
wants us to make better choices but He knows it requires
humility before we will choose His way. Humility means we
know that we don't know best, but God does.

We exercise humility when we commit to learning
what God says, what His Word instructs us to do, and by

praying about our decisions and then obeying Him no matter what we feel like doing.

When we lack humility, it deprives us of the ability to receive correction and discipline. It keeps us tied up in self deception. Proverbs 10:17 contrasts the person who cannot receive correction with the humble person in the following way: *"People who accept discipline are on the pathway to life, but those who ignore correction will go astray"* (Prov 10:17 NLT).

When we lack humility, we tend to disobey God and make poor choices. Perhaps we

- speak when we shouldn't
- say what we shouldn't
- don't say what we should
- watch, read and listen to what we shouldn't
- do the wrong things with the wrong people
- spend money on the wrong things
- hold on to anger and offense when we should forgive
- complain when we should be thankful
- think we know better than God
- think we will get away with all of the above.

The rewards of choosing to be humble and obeying God cannot be outdone by any other method or scheme you can come up with. James 4:9 exhorts us to

> ... *Be deeply penitent and grieve, even weep [over your disloyalty]. Let your laughter be turned to grief and your mirth to dejection and heartfelt shame [for your sins]. Humble yourselves [feeling very insignificant] in the presence of the Lord, and He will exalt you [He will lift you up and make your lives significant]*
>
> *James 4:9-10 AMP*

"By humility and fear of the Lord are riches honor and life."

Proverbs 22:4 NKJV

God's will is that you choose humility so He can make you great! Can you think of any reason not to choose humility at this point? Start practicing humility on purpose today.

Chapter 31

OBEDIENCE

*Be watchful and obey all these words which I
command you, that it may go well with you and with your
children after you forever, when you do what is good and
right in the sight of the Lord your God.*

DEUTERONOMY 12:28 AMP

Obedience seems simple: it's just doing what we should,
right? Unfortunately life frequently presents us with
situations that make obedience seem difficult and
complicated. For instance, what is the obedient thing to do
when a spouse doesn't do what they promised they would?
Should we say something? Should we remind them? Should
we say nothing? Do we just ignore our feelings of
disappointment? The Bible says in Colossians 3:18-19 that
wives should respect their husbands and husbands should
lovetheir wives, so what is the obedient thing for a husband
or a wife to do in such circumstances?

Often there is a gaping chasm between what we feel like doing and what we know we should do. I've discovered that most people mess up their lives and relationships by making the decision to go with their feelings on a daily basis. When we choose to go with our feelings of anger, frustration and resentment in dealing with our spouses, we are choosing to disobey God. Obeying God does not mean

Disobedience will always bring us to a difficult place.

that there will never be an opportunity to address and resolve the problem. Obeying God shows that we trust Him to show us how to resolve things in a way that will not only fix the current issue but will, at the same time, build and strengthen communication and trust within the relationship.

When we choose to disobey we give Satan an open door to come into our lives and bring destruction. Disobedience is sin. Sin is expensive in every way, and it costs us in our relationships, finances, and health. Disobedience will always bring us to a difficult place. To remain in disobedience is to sabotage God's very best plan for your life. It ensures that the destructive cycles in your life will continue. Obedience brings a blessing, disobedience a curse. God's blessings are conditional on our obedience. Obeying God brings the best outcome every time, even if it takes us through the difficult territory of going against what our feelings dictate.

Parents know the joy they experience when their child obeys happily the first time he is asked to do something. Because he obeys so readily they know that child can be trusted and they will want to bless him every chance they get.

What about the child that is surly and ignores the parents' requests repeatedly? Disobedience does not earn him favor or trust. This child is making the choice to earn disapproval. How confident will you be as a parent in giving this child the car keys when he reaches driving age, compared to the obedient one?

This little example illustrates the importance of obedience toward God. God wants to bless us, but our own acts of defiance show that we cannot be trusted to use His blessings in the right way.

There is always a reason why we find ourselves out of the will of God for our lives. It's called disobedience. The sin of disobedience blocks us from receiving what we need from God. Obedience on the other hand, opens up the channels so we can receive freely. Obedience gives us the confidence to hear from God and receive answers to our prayers.

> **The sin of disobedience blocks us from receiving what we need from God. Obedience opens up the channels so we can receive freely.**

Putting aside all compromise in our lives will give us hope in God's future plans for us. When we do this, God plants us back in the centre of His will and shows us how to make the most of the time we lost while in disobedience. The amazing thing is that *"God causes everything to work together for the good of those who love God and are called according to his purpose for them"* (Romans 8:28 NLT).

Obedience to God's Word brings His power into our lives and situations. Obedience also brings His blessings and favour. God's favour and blessing re-arranges our lives, putting everything in the right place.

What are the areas of your life where you are struggling to obey God? If you are still holding on to some areas of disobedience that you've identified in previous chapters, you need to ask yourself what is really holding you back. Remember, God doesn't need our strength to accomplish His will on the earth; He needs our obedience and submission to His will and plan. It seems He is just waiting to be good to us! In Deuteronomy Joshua tells the often disobedient Israelites,

> *And the Lord your God will make you abundantly*
> *prosperous in every work of your hand, in the fruit of*
> *your body, of your cattle, of your land, for good; for the*
> *Lord will again delight in prospering you, as He took*
> *delight in your fathers, If you obey the voice of the*
> *Lord your God, to keep His commandments and His*
> *statutes which are written in this Book of the Law,*
> *and if you turn to the Lord your God with all your*
> *[mind and] heart and with all your being. For this*
> *commandment which I command you this day is not*
> *too difficult for you, nor is it far off.*
>
> *Deuteronomy 30:9-11 AMP*

It's God's will for you to prosper! You may not need a miracle to change your life after all. All it takes to turn things around is to start obeying!

Chapter 32

CONFIDENCE

This is the confidence we have in approaching God:
that if we ask anything according to his will, he hears us.

1 JOHN 5:14 NIV

I am sure we have all experienced those days when things go particularly well. The future seems sunny and bright, and there is no challenge we feel we can't rise up to. That's the kind of confidence we can have every day when we believe in God's goodness, know His will, and act on it. If you've ever tried to give up a bad habit, you may remember that every time you did the right thing, your confidence in your ability to succeed seemed to grow.

Having confidence in our relationship with God requires knowing who He is, that His will for us is good, and then subsequently doing it. Some people have this backwards and wait to feel right before they do right. They may wait for a very long time!

Guilt and unbelief are attitudes that can really attack our confidence. If you have been taking serious inventory in the previous chapters, you have likely made good headway in terms of understanding and removing beliefs that have been holding you back. You will also better understand the difference between legitimate guilt that comes as a result of disobeying God and then leads to repentance, and the guilt from your former programming that robs you of your confidence in God and keeps you from pursuing your dreams and destiny.

When you lack confidence it causes you to second-guess your decisions and doubt your ability to hear from God. It robs you of the faith you need to make right decisions and reach your potential. To reiterate, *you* are in control of what you do with these negative feelings. Are you going to entertain them and allow them to keep a stranglehold on your life, or are you going to defeat them by telling yourself the truth of what God says about you? Solomon tells us that *"Guilt is banished through love and truth; Fear-of-God deflects evil"* (Prov. 16:6 MSG).

When guilt or unbelief become the basis of your decisions they will keep you out of the will of God, at times causing you to do things you don't even desire to do. Whether you're being pressured into buying something you don't need or being guilted into going against what you know to be God's will, you are inviting

> **Your will find the confidence you need to achieve your God-given destiny when you are utterly convinced it is God's will for you to succeed.**

problems. The fear of not pleasing others is a trap that's easy to fall into; it robs you of confidence and makes you easy prey for manipulators. A confident person knows when it's okay to say no. Confidence keeps us from falling into man-made traps and keeps us focused on our God-given goals. Again Proverbs warns us of that *"fear of man will prove to be a snare, but whoever trusts in the LORD is kept safe"* (Prov. 29:25 NIV).

You will find the confidence you need to achieve your God-given destiny when you are utterly convinced it is God's will for you to succeed. Some believers coming from a religious background need to be convinced that success is okay with God, while some prosperity minded Christians need to learn that success doesn't just fall on them because they claim it. Living righteously means allowing God to work through us, doing what He says to do, when He says to do it.

Whatever we do in our own strength brings no glory to Him and only trouble to us. The consequences of placing confidence in ourselves rather than in God are not very appealing! Proverbs calls the self-confident person a fool whose *"lips bring contention... [whose]mouth is his ruin, and [whose] lips are a snare to himself"* (Prov. 18: 6-7 AMP). Remember, the idea is to place our confidence not in ourselves, but in God.

The way we build the kind of confidence that we need for God to hear our prayers is to first hear what He tells us, believe what He says, and finally act on His Word.

Confidence in God brings hope which causes us to focus on thankfulness and praise, which in turn increases our level of faith. It results in a great cycle of thinking and believing we can choose to live in!

It is God's will that you be completely confident in His love for you and His great plan for your life. Don't let guilt or feelings of unworthiness rob you of your destiny by stealing your confidence. We've all messed up and done wrong things but it's no reason to stay stuck when God has given us a way to be free through Jesus. We can move forward in confidence when we know that we are in God's will. Make sure your words reflect your confidence in seeing God's promises becoming a reality. When this confidence comes across in words and actions, things begin to change for the better. The Psalmist asserts this belief in God's promises in Psalm 27:13:

> *"I am still confident of this: I will see the goodness of the LORD in the land of the living."*
>
> *Psalm 27:13 NIV*

Focus your mind on scriptures that specifically address your needs and concerns. Meditate on those words by reading, listening and confessing them throughout the day until you are completely confident that God can be trusted to provide the solution.

Chapter 33

BALANCE & BOUNDARIES

*The blessing of the Lord makes a person rich, and he
adds no sorrow with it.*

PROVERBS 10:22 NLT

When it comes down to finding balance and establishing
boundaries in life, what we don't do is as important as what
we actually do. If we have been given knowledge of how
God wants us to live from day to day, if we have gained
understanding of His purpose for us yet choose to live
outside of His will, we will be out of balance in all areas of
life to some degree, and will be unable to set proper
boundaries as a result.

Almost everyone has experienced a measure of
success in some way at some time, but for one reason or
another, success in other areas seems completely elusive.
Finding balance and establishing boundaries God's way is
the only way success in every area is possible. For instance,
someone can experience great success in ministry but

without God's wisdom there may be a tendency to put an unbalanced amount of time, energy and effort into it, meaning that someone or something elsewhere is being neglected, usually health or family relationships.

Whether we over-work or work too little, over-eat or under-eat, over-protect or neglect, oversleep or don't get enough sleep, over-react or back down too easily, over-achieve or under-achieve, we are shifting every other area of life out of balance and that will eventually have a consequence we don't want to deal with.

Finding balance and establishing boundaries God's way is the only way success in every area is possible.

Proverbs warns us to be wise enough to know when to quit: *"Don't wear yourself out trying to get rich. Be wise enough to know when to quit"* (Prov 23:4 NLT).

Whether we are putting too much time and energy into trying to get rich, trying to have the perfect body, the fanciest house, or the smartest kids, we have to remember that too much focus on one aspect of life leads to neglect of others. There is folly in extremes that we need to avoid. Finding the balance is key to avoiding many problems.

When we discover our purpose and begin to live it out in a balanced way remembering to respect the boundaries of others, we find satisfaction in our lives that we previously sought from other sources. God hasn't made it difficult to find His purpose for our lives; He wants us all to live it.

The lies we have allowed ourselves to believe are responsible for sending us into cycles of confusion. This cycle includes choosing compromising behavior, giving in to things we shouldn't (things that will eventually bring destruction into our lives), and then choosing compromise again. Whether it is poor lifestyle habits or wrong boundaries in relationships, we need to understand that this isn't God's will for us. We usually choose the wrong things because we haven't trusted God to completely satisfy our needs and desires.

Setting things straight often seems more difficult in our minds than it is in reality. Most of us know what is best, we just haven't correctly applied the knowledge yet. The answer may begin with merely changing one thing, a simple attitude or habit. Did you know that some people overeat when they are tired? Perhaps an earlier bedtime could be part of the answer to losing weight.

Could learning to say "no" to certain people and no longer being a people-pleaser be the answer to resolving stressful relationships and low self-esteem? In some cases being out of balance and not having proper boundaries in relationships can be a form of idolatry. We are to be God-pleasers, not people-pleasers.

In some cases being out of balance and not having proper boundaries in relationships can be a form of idolatry.

God is pleased when we obey Him because that is when we will be our strongest, happiest and most effective. His reasons for wanting our cooperation with His plan are because He knows and wants what is absolutely best for us.

God knows that an understanding of proper boundaries in relationships will prevent unnecessary conflict, frustration and resentment. We actually empower another's weaknesses when we continually rescue them from their poor choices. We are not responsible for another's irresponsible choices, even when they directly affect us. We risk stunting spiritual and emotional growth in others by repeatedly getting between them and the consequences of their choices. We are only responsible for our own response to the effects of their choices and behaviors on us.

When boundaries have become blurred by repeated violation through abuse or co-dependency, or by repeatedly doing for someone what they are capable of and should be doing for themselves, we only serve to empower their weaknesses. If we are still wiping a physically capable child's nose when he's ten, or still tying an eight-year-old's shoe laces, we are hampering their emotional and physical development because learning to master skills is a vital part of healthy growth.

A peculiar interplay happens when someone refuses to take their legitimate responsibility. Whether it is a husband or child dropping socks on the floor instead of putting them in the laundry hamper, or a wife racking up the credit cards, the guilty party is putting pressure on someone else to pay for their irresponsibility in some way. This seriously complicates relationships. Interestingly enough, the responsible person's efforts are seldom appreciated and they are often accused of being controlling!

Re-establishing healthy boundaries begins by taking appropriate responsibility for our own life and choices while stepping back to let others take ownership of theirs. God's Word is the guide for establishing the right boundaries and balance in every area. When we depend on worldly knowledge to show us balance and boundaries we will be constantly confused because worldly rules keep changing. Just think of how many diet programs there are out there! Even though some diets seem good and practical it won't be five minutes until you find another that contradicts the first. God's Word is to be the first and final word if you are to live confidently and wisely. He designed your body to tell you when it needs fuel or sleep. It also tells you when it's had enough! God's Word has all the wisdom and knowledge we need to overcome negative or destructive patterns, we just need to trust Him. Consider the following wise counsel from Proverbs as it pertains to trusting God for the wisdom to help us establish healthy behaviours:

Trust God from the bottom of your heart; don't try to figure out everything on your own. Listen for God's voice in everything you do, everywhere you go; He's the one who will keep you on track. Don't assume that you know it all. Run to God! Run from evil! Your body will glow with health, your very bones will vibrate with life!

Proverbs 3:5 MSG

We will never be wise enough to successfully live a balanced life without God. It is His will that we seek Him every day for His wisdom and direction in all areas of life.

Chapter 34

BRAD'S STORY

Brad was in a desperate state when I first met him. His wife of almost 20 years wanted out of the marriage, and he hated that he was losing control. He couldn't seem to do anything to stop her leaving. But he tried, mostly by employing guilt. When a controller begins to sense they are losing control, things begin to look very ugly. Brad lost his filter for when it was okay to call people and talk about his troubles. He thought nothing of calling people in the middle of the night, several times leaving messages at half hour intervals. He was so wrapped up in his own feelings that he had no regard for anyone else's.

This was the crisis that years of this couple's bad choices had been leading up to. Brad had huge anger and control issues and he could no longer hide them, even though he continued to try denying them for a while. Not only had the marriage failed, but Brad was also in serious danger of losing his kids and home.

This was the first of many difficult things Brad had to admit to about his own behaviour. Brad had been raised in the church and continued this tradition with his own family. As he began to see the truth about God's will for him as a husband and father he knew he was in the wrong and without excuses. Because he'd previously failed to trust God with his relationships, he had resorted to using intimidation and control. By doing this Brad reaped destruction instead of blessing. Brad began to discover that church attendance and obedience to God was not the same thing.

Brad's first step of humility came when he began admitting that his problems were his and his alone. No matter what his wife had done wrong, nothing changed the fact that he had been angry and controlling throughout their marriage. He had trusted in his own strength, not God's.

The initial changes in him were remarkable. He went from being loud, intense, bitter, angry, and complaining about his problems to anyone who would listen (actually most were not really willing listeners just people who were cornered and couldn't escape), to a man who learned to listen and encourage others. People no longer try to escape when they see Brad, because his focus is no longer on himself. He now has two-way conversations.

There were many issues Brad had to deal with which he humbly tackled one by one:

- He admitted the effect his verbal abuse had on his children, and sought their forgiveness.
- He admitted he enjoyed the sympathy and support he got by gossiping about his wife.
- He let go of his right to blame and complain about his wife's behaviour.
- He took responsibility for the debt they had incurred during the marriage. He started living on a budget and within his means for the first time.

Brad made obeying God his number one priority. At this point he has read through the Bible four times.

The result three years later is that Brad's relationship with his children is better than ever; his three youngest children live with him. For the first time in his life Brad is a home owner. One year after his divorce God brought a wonderful Christian woman into his life. Brad continues to experience God's blessing in his life because of his choice to be humble and obedient.

Part Six

Exposing your Purpose

*If any man has ears to hear, let him be
listening and let him perceive and comprehend.
And He said to them, Be careful what you are
hearing. The measure of thought [and study] you
give [to the truth you hear] will be the measure [of
virtue and knowledge] that comes back to you - and
more [besides] will be given to you who hear.
Mark 4:23-24 AMP*

Chapter 35

SOWING & REAPING

*In the morning sow your seed, and in the evening do not
withhold your hand, for you do not know which will
prosper, either this or that, or whether both alike will be
good.*

ECCLESIASTES 11:6 NKJV

We are all the result of a seed being sown. Our thoughts
are the result of seeds of information that have been sown
into our minds. As we discussed earlier, these seeds are
nurtured and become rooted in our belief system when we
meditate on them. When mature, the fruit of planted seeds
pours out of our mouths and is evidenced in our
behaviour. We will sow whatever seeds we possess,
whether they are good seeds of godly knowledge (i.e.
kindness, love, faith) or evil seeds of hatred, anger,
bitterness, strife and selfishness. We will also harvest those
same seeds in our own lives in the future.

When the harvest comes, we may not easily recognize the fruit. Does an acorn resemble an oak tree or an apple seed an apple? Not in the least! If you hadn't been taught these facts you might never make the connection. Life is like that: at times we sow evil seeds then start praying for a crop failure! It's not easy to see or admit that we have something to do with the destructive forces at work in our lives and circumstances, but the following verses make it clear that we do:

> *Do not be deceived: God cannot be mocked. A man reaps what he sows. The one who sows to please his sinful nature, from that nature will reap destruction; the one who sows to please the Spirit, from the Spirit will reap eternal life. Let us not become weary in doing good, for at the proper time we will reap a harvest if we do not give up (Gal 6:7-9 NIV).*

It's really not so complicated when you think about it. If you sow tomatoes, you'll reap tomatoes! While this verse shows us one way we bring destruction into our lives, the following verse again affirms that God has given us the means to find a way out of destruction through the healing, restoring and renewing knowledge and power of His Word: *"He sent His word and healed them, and delivered them from their destructions"* (Psalm 107:20 NKJV).

Throughout this book we have been identifying the lies that we've believed, and been encouraged to replace them with God's words of truth. God's words have power to heal and deliver. This is the process God uses to save us from further self-imposed destruction. In the book of Hosea we learn that God's people were being destroyed because of the truth they didn't know. God lamented to His prophet, *"My people are destroyed from lack of knowledge"* (Hosea 4:6 NIV).

These days we have no excuse for not having God's knowledge since most of us have several versions of the Bible in our homes! Even during the days of Hosea God was holding people responsible for the seeds they sowed in their lives. He said to His people,

> *Sow for yourselves according to righteousness (uprightness and right standing with God); reap according to mercy and loving-kindness. Break up your uncultivated ground, for it is time to seek the Lord, to inquire for and of Him, and to require His favor, till He comes and teaches you righteousness and rains His righteous gift of salvation upon you. You have plowed and plotted wickedness, you have reaped the [willful] injustice [of oppressors], you have eaten the fruit of lies. Because you have trusted in your [own] way and your chariots, in the multitude of your mighty men (Hosea 10:12-13 AMP).*

It's up to us to decide what we know and sow.

In previous chapters you've learned about the power that is available to you over your own thoughts, deeds and behaviors. Your behaviour changes as your knowledge and thinking changes. When your behaviour changes, so do your results (or harvest). Proverbs warns us that, *"He who sows iniquity will reap sorrow"* (Prov. 22:8 NKJV).

It also helps to understand that it's not just the kind of seeds we sow that are important. In order to get the best possible harvest we also have to learn to sow them in the right ground.

Let's think of our time, love and effort as seeds. If we sow marital love seeds into adulterous ground, the harvest is devastating to our spouse and family. If we sow marital time and love seeds into the ground of our children, parents, friends or work, our marriage relationship will suffer and be off balance. If your choices cause one area to be off balance, all other areas will be negatively affected. We may pamper or spoil our children,

In order to get the best possible harvest we also have to learn to sow them in the right ground.

or parents and friends may have too much input into our lives. If we give work priority, our spouses and children may become bitter and resentful.

Think about money as seeds for a moment. What happens when you sow your money into things you cannot afford instead of paying bills? You will eventually lack the necessities, and invite stress into your life. Stress plays a huge factor in your physical health, and impacts your relationships.

God has given us all the time we need to accomplish His purposes in our lives. We do possess enough time to make enough money to meet our needs, to nurture our relationships, and to fulfill His call on our lives. We cannot keep all of these things in the proper balance without His wisdom. This is why people can be extremely successful in some area, but fail miserably in others.

We've likely all heard of couples whose goal was to pay off their mortgage in the shortest time possible. They often work several jobs and sacrifice many things to achieve this seemingly worthy goal. Though they frequently succeed in quickly becoming mortgage-free, their marriages often pay the ultimate price and crumble in the process. In the end no one gets to enjoy the mortgage-free homes they sacrificed so much to have.

Everyone has the same twenty-four hours in a day; whether we spend this time wisely or not is up to us.

This is the type of destruction God wants to protect us from. God's Word is powerful and has the answers we need! What we do with the knowledge He gives us is up to us. Everyone has the same twenty-four hours in a day; whether we spend this time wisely or not is up to us. Our productivity and use of time very much depends on what we believe and value.

So far we have allowed God's Word to shed light on how we've invited destruction. We can now use these same principles to prevent further destruction and sow for the kind of harvest we want in the future. The apostle Paul was a strong believer in the concept of sowing and reaping, and understood the importance of persistence in sowing good seeds. This exhortation to the Galatian believers is still relevant to us today:

> *So let's not get tired of doing what is good. At just the right time we will reap a harvest of blessing if we don't give up. Therefore, whenever we have the opportunity, we should do good to everyone—especially to those in the family of faith (Gal. 6:9-10 NLT).*

When you have understanding of the principles of sowing and reaping you can direct your sowing very specifically. You can sow towards healthier relationships and better health and finances. You can sow towards your destiny by developing more skill in the area you feel called to serve. Decide what you can do daily to sow into your destiny.

You are the one who makes the choice what you sow, where you sow and how generously you sow. Your future harvest is in your hands!

> *[Remember] this: he who sows sparingly and grudgingly will also reap sparingly and grudgingly, and he who sows generously [that blessings may come to someone] will also reap generously and with blessings.*
>
> *2 Corinthians 9:6 AMP*

When we begin to think of everything we do and say as a seed, it will change the way we live.

Chapter 36

FAITH

But without faith it is impossible to please and be satisfactory to Him. For whoever would come near to God must [necessarily] believe that God exists and that He is the rewarder of those who earnestly and diligently seek Him [out].

HEBREWS 11:6 AMP

Without faith we cannot fulfill the plan of God for our life, or experience His rewards. Faith comes from knowing God's ways and believing His words. Every day we put faith in things and people that will eventually disappoint us. Even when we flip a light switch we have faith that it will turn on. We have experts telling us that something is good for us, only to have them admit they got it wrong later. It seems easier to put faith in things that we can see and touch, even when we know they can fail. As followers of God however, our faith does not *"rest in the wisdom of men (human philosophy), but in the power of God"* (1 Cor 2:5 AMP).

Even though God assures us that He will never let us down, we struggle with keeping our faith in Him strong. Foundational to a strong faith is to hear the Word of God in the first place (Rom 10:17).

We can easily access biblical teaching and determine what we allow in our ears. We need faith for every step of obedience with God. Without faith all our dreams are limited. Faith in God takes us to a level of believing for what we would otherwise find impossible or unachievable. Faith grows when we sow time, effort, and energy into it.

Faith in God takes us to a level of believing for what we would otherwise find impossible or unachievable.

Building and strengthening our faith is entirely up to us. We can choose to spend our time, effort, and energy on being discontent and worrying about how to fix our problems. This will develop the opposite of faith: fear and hopelessness. The right choice is to live by faith. In doing so our eyes are opened to all kinds of opportunities and possibilities. Faith puts action to our beliefs and gives us courage to step outside our comfort zone and do what needs to be done to see God's plans realized.

Throughout scripture Abraham is praised for being a man of faith. In an unbelievable act of faith Abraham was willing to sacrifice his only son – his promised son – because he believed in God's goodness and faithfulness. James tells us that *"his faith and his actions worked together. His actions made his faith complete"* (James 2:22 NLT).

Abraham's lesson gave us one of the greatest examples of laying down our own will and placing our faith completely in God.

Faith is the means to accomplish God-sized tasks. Faith is so powerful that it will rearrange your life by changing the way you think, feel and act. We can produce an environment for our faith and vision to grow by choosing to get involved with the right people and influences. Our vision will thrive under the right faith-building conditions.

If we refuse to do what it takes to grow in faith we are saying "no" to God's plan for our success. Living by faith means we don't wait for perfect conditions to do what needs to be done; we do it just because God said so! There is a nugget of wisdom in Ecclesiastes that says, *"He who observes the wind [and waits for all conditions to be favorable] will not sow, and he who regards the clouds will not reap"* (Eccl 11:4 AMP). A loose modern-day translation may be, "get off your butt and do (sow) something already!"

> **Living by faith means we don't wait for perfect conditions to do what needs to be done; we do it just because God said so!**

The Bible tells the story of a woman with the issue of blood who gathered up the faith to just touch Jesus' robe so she could be healed. There was nothing about the conditions that were in her favor. She'd spent twelve years and a lot of money looking for the cure for her condition, but her suffering continued. Without faith she would have given up. The Bible tells us that she kept saying, "if only I can touch His garment, I shall be restored to health." After she had touched His robe in faith, we read:

> *And immediately her flow of blood was dried up at the source, and [suddenly] she felt in her body that she was healed of her [distressing] ailment. And Jesus, recognizing in Himself that the power proceeding from Him had gone forth, turned around immediately in the crowd and said, "Who touched My clothes?" And the disciples kept saying to Him, "You see the crowd pressing hard around You from all sides, and You ask, Who touched Me?" Still He kept looking around to see her who had done it. But the woman, knowing what had been done for her, though alarmed and frightened and trembling, fell down before Him*

*and told Him the whole truth. And He said to her,
"Daughter, your faith (your trust and confidence in
Me, springing from faith in God) has restored you to
health. Go in [into] peace and be continually healed
and freed from your [distressing bodily] disease"
(Mark 5:24-34 AMP).*

This woman was single-minded and sure – that's how faith works! She decided what to believe and acted on it. She could have missed the opportunity for her healing if she hadn't. She was so filled with faith for her healing that she knew beyond doubt that just touching Jesus' garment was enough. She didn't even need Him to speak to her or touch her! Her faith was like the one described in Hebrews as being *"the confidence that what we hope for will actually happen, [giving] us the assurance about things we cannot see"* (Hebrews 11:1 NLT).

It was her faith in His ability to heal that gave her confidence to show up and push through that crowd. Without faith she may have stayed home like many others did, wallowing in her sad history of failure, telling herself she'd already tried everything so there was no point. Hearing about Jesus and His miracles expanded her vision of being healed while her growing faith gave her the courage to act. Having faith means we can't be double-minded and doubting; having faith doesn't allow us to give up. James talks about this kind of persistent faith when asking for wisdom:

*If you need wisdom, ask our generous God, and he
will give it to you. He will not rebuke you for asking.
But when you ask him, be sure that your faith is in
God alone. Do not waver, for a person with divided
loyalty is as unsettled as a wave of the sea that is
blown and tossed by the wind. Such people should not
expect to receive anything from the Lord. Their loyalty
is divided between God and the world, and they are
unstable in everything they do (James 1:5-8 NLT).*

The woman who met Jesus had obviously heard about Him before He showed up in her area. She would have heard about the things He was saying and doing, so by the time He got there she was so filled with what she'd heard that nothing was going to stop her. She expected to receive healing and she did! Whatever your need may be, that kind of faith will take you where the need will be met. Jesus assures us, *"whatever you ask for in prayer, having faith and [really] believing, you will receive"*(Matt 21:22 AMP).

Another tool to help build and strengthen your faith is to surround yourself with people who can believe with and for you. If you don't have people like that in your life, be intent on finding some. When Jesus was performing miracles it wasn't always the individual needing the miracle who had the faith for it. Look at the guy whose four friends fought their way through a crowd and ripped off the roof of someone's house to get him his healing. Don't let your faith be limited by anyone or anything; you can't please God without it.

Let your roots grow down into him, and let your lives be built on him. Then your faith will grow strong in the truth you were taught, and you will overflow with thankfulness.

Colossians 2:7 NLT

Just like the woman who sought out Jesus you need to become so filled up with stories of what God has done and what He wants to do that nothing will stop you from taking action!

Chapter 37

LOVE

*If I could speak all the languages of earth and of
angels, but didn't love others, I would only be a noisy
gong or a clanging cymbal. If I had the gift of
prophecy, and if I understood all of God's secret plans
and possessed all knowledge, and if I had such faith that
I could move mountains, but didn't love others, I
would be nothing. If I gave everything I have to the
poor and even sacrificed my body, I could boast about it;
but if I didn't love others, I would have gained
nothing.*

1 CORINTHIANS 13:1-3 NLT

We have covered many topics so far – some highlighted
issues we needed to deal with, others pointed out what we
can do to change – but this chapter on love is really the
defining chapter for all of us. The verse you've just read
basically says that even if you do everything you've learned

so far correctly, love must be your motivation or you are just wasting your time and making lots of noise over nothing. Love is the greatest force in the universe.

According to Scripture, there are three things that last forever – faith, hope, and love. Of these, love is the greatest (1 Cor. 13:13). The Beatles said it back in the 60's: "All you need is love." There is truth to that, but only if you're clear about what love is.

There certainly is a lot of love around. People love much, but often it's the object of their love that is the problem. People love their cars, their houses, their food and themselves. They talk about these things so passionately that you know it's real. The problem with sowing all that loving in the wrong place is that the results will not be good, because it's sowing to the flesh. Literally, people who love food too much will reap destruction in their bodies; people who love their stuff too much will reap destruction in the form of debt. People who love themselves more than anyone else will end up with the object of their affection: alone. The list could go on but the results of loving the wrong things speak for themselves.

> **People love much, but often it's the object of their love that is the problem.**

God talks about a different kind of love, a love that is not wrapped up in having our selfish needs met but instead focuses on loving God first, and then others. In fact, Jesus tells us that love is the most important commandment of all:

> *Jesus replied, "The most important commandment is this: 'Listen, O Israel! The Lord our God is the one and only Lord. And you must love the Lord your God with all your heart, all your soul, all your mind, and all your strength.' The second is equally important: 'Love your neighbor as yourself.' No other*

commandment is greater than these" (Mark 12:29-31 NLT).

Think about it, if you love God you'll want to do what is right. If you love your neighbour the way you love yourself, chances are you won't steal from him, kill him, talk badly about him or hurt his wife and kids. Thinking of it this way is easier than running through the list of Ten Commandments before deciding what to do. Love is the great simplifier, if we don't try to complicate it!

What scares most people about loving the way God does is that they may end up having to do things they don't want to do. They're right - we get no credit for loving just when we feel like it! There is no effort or sacrifice in that since we are simply doing what we want. Jesus addressed this self-seeking "love" by saying,

> *If you love only those who love you, why should you get credit for that? Even sinners love those who love them! And if you do good only to those who do good to you, why should you get credit? Even sinners do that much! (Luke 6:32-33 NLT).*

Simply put, the kind of love God is looking for is simply to love others in the ways you yourself desire to be loved. It's the Golden Rule we teach our children:

Do to others as you would like them to do to you.

(Luke 6:31 NLT)

Let's think about what that would look like for a moment. For one thing we'd want to be loved unconditionally, and not because of what we do or don't do. We'd want people to help us in whatever way we needed help when we needed it. We'd want to be appreciated, included, and accepted, we would not want to be gossiped about, rejected or judged, right?

To love without conditions is to be attentive and responsive to the needs of those God places in your path, even if it's only for a few moments at the checkout. It's doesn't mean preaching to them, it means considering their needs and concerns before your own. It means addressing the fears of the people around you in a way that brings them peace and hope.

If we want to live under God's blessing, we have to walk in love. No plan works right unless selfless love is the motivation behind it. Not faith, not giving, not your words and not your actions. Love is the most powerful force that exists. To me, the most amazing thing about love is that it never fails to accomplish its purpose!

Ultimately, each of us will be defined by the way we did or did not love. The world's most admired and loved figures are not remembered because of being rich or famous, but because of their loving acts. Mother Theresa is a household name because of the way she loved. By dedicating her life to the poor, she showed us one of the best modern-day examples of walking in love. Even people who don't know God can't help but respond when they witness the kind of love we read about in Corinthians 13:

> **Ultimately, each of us will be defined by the way we did or did not love.**

Love is patient and kind. Love is not jealous or boastful or proud or rude. It does not demand its own way. It is not irritable, and it keeps no record of being wronged. It does not rejoice about injustice but rejoices whenever the truth wins out. Love never gives up, never loses faith, is always hopeful, and endures through every circumstance (1 Cor 13:4-7).

Love is the answer to your fears. God's love casts out fear because it's perfect and always has your best in mind.

The gifts and personality traits you discovered earlier are merely indicators of how God has designed you to show His love to the world in a unique way - a way that only you can. When you allow Him to, He connects your experiences to your unique gifts and personality, and He shows you how to communicate His love through them. You will never be more satisfied than when you are in the centre of God's will, loving the way you've been created to.

> *"Above all, clothe yourselves with love, which binds us all together in perfect harmony."*
>
> *Colossians 3:14 NLT*

Think about ways you can change your "love life" today. Success is guaranteed!

Chapter 38

SUCCESS

This Book of the Law shall not depart out of your mouth, but you shall meditate on it day and night, that you may observe and do according to all that is written in it. For then you shall make your way prosperous, and then you shall deal wisely and have good success.

JOSHUA 1:8 AMP

Some Christians have strange reactions to the word "success." Some fear that success means focusing on money or selfish achievement. The reality is that focusing on finding success is indeed a legitimate concern if it's all about what you want. If your plan for success lines up with God's, you won't have to worry about it. God wants all of us to succeed in what He has called us to do. His purpose for each one of us is different. For one, success may mean a platform, reaching a place of great influence and wealth. For another it may mean funding orphanages in third world countries, or rescuing children from sex slave traders. For others, success will be raising a godly family and paying the bills on time. Jesus completed His mission successfully: it was to die on the cross so mankind could be reconciled to God. There is no limit to the ways we can experience success. Proverbs tells us that when we commit our works to God, He will cause our thoughts to become agreeable to His will and our plans will succeed (Prov 16:3 AMP).

For Christians, success can be summed up in the following way:

- Knowing what the Word says
- Understanding how to live it
- Believing that God is faithful to His word
- Obediently doing what it says in faith and love
- Experiencing prosperity and success as a result

God had many successful people serving Him throughout Scripture. He didn't seem to concern Himself about how much or how little they possessed. Abraham, Moses, David and Joseph had a lot of possessions and wealth, but they never let it get between them and their love for God. There were others like John the Baptist and Jesus' disciples who had little in the way of material possessions, but they didn't let this get between them and their love for God either. Success clearly has little to do with how much or how little we possess. It's about reaching our potential and fulfilling our purpose.

Success is not accidental. It's committing to God's process of transformation by obeying Him. He then takes what we've learned from the experiences we've gone through, adds it to the gifts, personality traits and desires we have and uses it to help heal and restore others through us. In short, success is keeping the goal of pleasing God in mind, and then sowing the right things in the right place to get the right results.

Listen carefully to what I am saying—and be wary of the shrewd advice that tells you how to get ahead in the world on your own. Giving, not getting, is the way. Generosity begets generosity. Stinginess impoverishes.

Mark 4:24-25 MSG

You are successful when you are using the best of who you are to help those who need it most.

Chapter 39

FREE WILL

Teach me to do your will, for you are my God.

May your gracious Spirit lead me forward on a firm footing.

PSALM 143:10 NLT

Life can seem very unfair when we don't understand free will. Exercising your free will by surrendering it to God's will is the most powerful weapon for life change. Free will is the ability to choose what we want to believe, do, say and think. We exercise our free will every time we make a choice, even when we decide to obey God rather than our own feelings.

Free will allows us to hold on to things we feel we have a right to, even when it hurts us. For example, free will gives us,

- The right to be angry
- The right to be lazy

- The right to be depressed
- The right to fail
- The right to waste our resources

Realize that we take our wrong attitudes and dysfunctional behavior with us everywhere we go. External changes will not cut it in the long run. Jesus does not want to merely adjust our behaviour. His plan is for our total transformation which ultimately changes the way we exercise our free will.

Genuine internal change becomes most evident to others through our changed behavior - our different reactions to certain stimulus or stressful events and situations. If people are looking for evidence of real change, they will see it in those moments when we would normally react wrongly, perhaps by losing our cool, complaining or arguing. They know our old triggers, our conditioned reactions. Only consistently different responses are proof to others of a changed life. The more we practice by submitting our will to God's in moments of decision, the more consistent they become.

> **Jesus does not want to merely adjust our behaviour. His plan is for our total transformation which ultimately changes the way we exercise our free will.**

Changing our habitual reaction means making a different choice in the split seconds between stimulus and response. This is the moment of exercising our free will with the greatest impact and power for life change. When we become aware of our own destructive conditioned responses we can choose the appropriate reaction. For example, instead of giving an opinion or angry answer, we can give a gentle answer and turn away wrath (Prov. 15:1). Instead of responding or reacting to hurtful comments, we can choose to stay silent.

The biggest problem we have about free will is that the bad guys get to have it too. When people choose to live selfishly, without regard for God or others, it affects all of us in ways we don't like. Free will means we all get to make our own choices.

> *"For they hated knowledge and chose not to fear the Lord."*
>
> *Proverbs 1:29 NLT*

Exercise your free will in ways that are guaranteed to bring the results you want.

Chapter 40

HEATHER'S STORY

*M*y initial meeting with Heather came several months after she had separated from her husband of twenty years. She had already bought a home of her own and was well settled there with her children. She worked part-time in a corner store. Heather explained that she had been counting the days until she could escape from her loveless marriage for the previous three years.

Two things struck me in that first session. First, Heather was a sweet woman who really believed that somewhere out there her Prince Charming really existed and would be along any moment on his white horse to sweep her off her feet and finally make up for all those years of misery she'd endured. The second thing was that even though she was now living the life she'd been planning for years, she didn't appear to have any joy about it.

In subsequent sessions I also learned of her twenty year struggles with health issues, children, and finances. Rarely did she mention her husband by name. As we worked on her issues one by one, I noted that she was one of the most teachable people I'd ever met. Every week she would make notes during our session. When she would return the following week she would have done everything I'd suggested and then some! Her eagerness to learn, change and grow was palpable; the results of her efforts and diligence were remarkable and came so quickly, at times I had trouble keeping up!

We started with the issues in her thinking. As quickly as her perceptions and beliefs changed, her spending and relationships did too. As she set up healthier boundaries in her relationships, she quickly gained a new level of respect from her kids. Within weeks of giving up some toxic relationships, she was offered two dream jobs (one that she'd applied for, another from a place she'd been volunteering). Heather literally went from the corner store to two paid part-time positions in the social service field!

> **As quickly as her perceptions and beliefs changed, her spending and relationships did too.**

Heather was enjoying her relationship with God in ways she'd never before experienced, but there was still more to come. Even though her cup was overflowing from all the blessings that had come her way in the previous four months, there was more. Her healing came next. Heather innocently told me one day that her health issues were given to her by God to prepare her for the work she was now doing. Since this comment didn't settle too well with me, I suggested that she pray about this since something else could be to blame, such as interaction of different medications and vitamins. True to form she took the bull by the horns and found herself talking to a naturopathic pharmacist the next day. This pharmacist patiently listened to her twenty-year medical history, which included a multitude of food allergies. In the end, he told her that every symptom she'd described could be explained away by a misdiagnosed case of Candida twenty years previously. He recommended some probiotics and sent her on her way. Within two months, Heather was able to eat everything she'd previously had to avoid, her energy levels were up and her symptoms had disappeared.

People who knew her were being greatly impacted by the changes in her life and the speed at which things were changing. Heather was exercising her free will in a different way. She was no longer making choices according to her emotions in the moment. She had transformed her mind so that her choices now lined up with God's truth. In this she was completely radical; she didn't always even understand why a certain choice was better she just knew that if the Bible told her so, she was going to do it.

The biggest problem Heather had was extending her love and kindness to her own husband who had continued to hope for reconciliation. This was to be the biggest test of Heather's submission and obedience to God. Her faith had been greatly built during the previous months. She began to trust that it was possible for God to change her heart towards her husband too. Certainly there was no natural desire in her to do so. Heather reluctantly but obediently invited her husband to counseling with her. They were encouraged to take things very slowly so that she would not feel pressured. It seemed that God didn't want to wait to bless Heather's radical obedience and faith! Six weeks later God had turned Heather's heart and marriage around miraculously and completely.

A few things set Heather apart which I believe played a huge part in the rate of her recovery and restoration. First, as I mention earlier, the speed at which she obeyed. Second, because her heart was so open and humble she easily set her ego aside. Heather quickly became aware of her own issues and took full responsibility for them. Third, she acted by faith on the truths she was learning. Finally, she naturally seemed to extend unconditional love and acceptance to everyone she met. Her career took her in the direction of caring for pregnant teens as well as the mentally challenged, all of whom loved her. People of all ages gravitate to Heather as if there is some magnetic force, and really, there is!

Heather and her husband give all glory to God for the life they have today, a life free from the confusion, delusion, depression and bitterness that almost destroyed their marriage and family. The work that God has done in them and their family truly encourages and inspires others to see that nothing is impossible for God and He is true to His promises to restore, heal and renew.

Heather's story provides a wonderful example of what happens when one person becomes radically submitted to God's will!

Conclusion

EVERYTHING MATTERS

But don't just listen to God's word. You must do what it says. Otherwise, you are only fooling yourselves. For if you listen to the word and don't obey, it is like glancing at your face in a mirror. You see yourself, walk away, and forget what you look like. But if you look carefully into the perfect law that sets you free, and if you do what it says and don't forget what you heard, then God will bless you for doing it.

JAMES 1:22-25 (NLT)

I used to use the expression "it doesn't matter" quite often. But by now I have realized that everything really does matter. Everything we say, everything we do, everything we think and believe, even the things we should do but don't. Free will gives us authority over all these areas, but on our own we will never have enough wisdom to make the right choices consistently. We need a relationship with Jesus, the power of the Holy Spirit and

God's wisdom to equip and direct us to live the best life possible. Everything matters because every word, thought and action is a potential seed for success or failure, health or sickness, poverty or prosperity. Because everything really does matter, we know that every belief, word or action is a seed planted that will bring a harvest. Every day you are sowing into yourself and into others, you determine your harvest, and you can stop destruction. You are in charge of you.

Everything you put into your mind or heart or allow out of your mouth is not just thinking, doing or saying; it's planting, and the harvest will come. God knows when and what it will look like and whether it will bring blessing or pain. God is always working for our good. Time is probably the most valuable thing we have, and unlike other things, once it's gone it's gone, and cannot be replaced. God urges us to use our time wisely, beginning by taking time to plant His words of life and truth in our hearts where they can grow and produce the prosperous life He desires for us to live.

> **Everything you put into your mind or heart, or allow out of your mouth is not just thinking, doing or saying; it's planting, and the harvest will come.**

The choice to experience God's best is really up to each of us. It's up to us to acknowledge our own wrong choices and take responsibility for them. *Just Getting Over Yourself* empowers you by taking you beyond the thinking that has been constricted by ignorance, fear, selfishness and pride. When you get over yourself, you become aware of the possibilities and opportunities God puts before you each day. In God's kingdom there are no limits, it's the place where "all things are possible" when we believe the right things!

"Every word of God is pure; He is a shield unto them who put their trust in Him." Proverbs 30:5 NKJV

Notes

1. American Society of Plastic Surgeons. "Cosmetic and Reconstructive Plastic Surgery Trends." http://www.plasticsurgery.org/Documents/Media/statistics/2009quickfacts-cosmetic-surgery-minimally-invasice-statistics.pdf, 28 July 2010

40 Day Life Change Challenge
Sign up is FREE!

http://justgetoveryourself.com

Where will you be six months, one year or even five years from now if you don't commit to real change?

JUST GET OVER YOURSELF 40 day Life Change Challenge is like a boot camp for learning to think right and live great. To make it even more fun find some friends to take the challenge with you! All you need is a copy of the book.

Benefits:

You will receive Dig Deeper emails with questions to enhance your change experience and turbo charge your results.

Challenge graduates will also receive discounts on other available services.